The AI Muse

How Machines Are Redefining Creativity

by
Clara Vossler

The AI Muse

How Machines Are
Redefining Creativity

Contents

Introduction

In the modern landscape of creativity, a new force is making ripples across the artistic spectrum: Artificial Intelligence (AI). Long confined to the realm of science fiction, AI has transcended its roots, becoming a vibrant collaborator in the creative process. This transformation is not merely technological; it's philosophical, cultural, and deeply human. As AI embeds itself into the creative fold, it challenges our notions of art, design, and media, urging us to reconceptualize what creativity itself can be.

Creativity has always been a cornerstone of human identity. It's how we've built civilizations, expressed our deepest emotions, and communicated across time and space. Yet, as we stand on the brink of this digital revolution, AI is not just reshaping creative processes; it is redefining the creative frontier. The question is no longer if AI can be creative, but rather how it harnesses creativity to generate novel expressions that surprise even their own creators.

The introduction of AI into the creative industries is akin to the invention of the printing press or the camera—tools that democratized and transformed access to art and information. AI's potential reaches far beyond mere augmentation of human skill; it offers a new collaborative partner that can generate ideas we might never have envisioned. This partnership is beginning to erode the traditional barriers between artist and machine, offering a glimpse into a future where creative acts are the product of symbiotic unity rather than dichotomy.

However, as with any cultural shift, the integration of AI into the creative industries brings with it profound questions and challenges. We are urged to reflect on the essence of authorship and creativity. Who owns an AI-generated piece of art, and who can claim credit for an AI-composed symphony? These pressing inquiries push us to revisit age-old concepts of originality and authenticity in art, urging us to reconsider what constitutes artistic value and merit.

The ethical dimensions cannot be overlooked. AI's encroachment into domains traditionally dominated by human creativity provokes crucial discussions around creative sovereignty and the potential homogenization of artistic expression. What ethical frameworks do we need to develop to ensure that AI technologies enhance rather than diminish cultural diversity and human expression?

Beyond ethical and philosophical concerns lies the economic impact. The business models of creative industries are evolving rapidly in response to AI's capabilities. As industries strive to integrate AI more into their workflows, there is an increasing realization of the transformative potential AI brings to market dynamics. Companies are beginning to monetize AI-driven creativity, setting new standards for efficiency and personalization. The interplay between creativity and commerce is being redefined, presenting opportunities for innovators and challenges for those who must adapt.

AI's involvement in creativity is more than technology adoption; it is a metamorphosis of process and perception. It cultivates a mindset where limitations are merely another parameter to be explored—another boundary to be transcended. Through AI, we are urged to engage with a new dialect of creativity, one that demands collaborative innovation and imaginative courage.

This book aims to provide a comprehensive perspective on AI's burgeoning role in culture and creativity. It's structured to guide you through the early history of AI in art, its present influence across varied domains, and speculates on its future trajectory. Each chapter delves into specific intersections of AI with various creative fields, offering insights into the synergies and tensions that arise from this unprecedented collaboration.

The exploration of AI in creativity also raises intriguing philosophical questions about the nature of creativity and consciousness. Can machines possess what we term as 'creative spark,' or is their output merely a sophisticated imitation of human innovation? The inquiry extends beyond the practical applications of AI and touches the core of human identity and consciousness.

Furthermore, the influence of AI in creativity is not confined to one location; it is a global phenomenon that impacts cultures differently. Chapters dedicated to regional perspectives highlight how AI-driven creativity adapts and evolves in diverse cultural landscapes, facilitating global collaborations in art and design. This diversity demonstrates not just the adaptability of AI but also its potential to enrich global cultural exchanges.

Through a series of case studies, this book showcases successful AI art projects and the lessons learned from pioneering artists. These case studies serve as a testament to the growing acceptance and integration of AI technologies in creative practices worldwide. They highlight both the capabilities and limitations of what can be achieved when human imagination meets machine intelligence.

Ultimately, AI's role in creativity is a dialogic process: a conversation between the impassive logic of machines and the subjective nuances of human experience. This discourse compels us to redefine what it means to create and how we perceive the works of creativity that populate our world. As AI continues to push the boundaries of what's possible, it invites us to embrace a future where creativity knows no limits, only opportunities.

The following pages aim to inspire, educate, and challenge. They provide a roadmap for navigating the confluence of AI and creativity, encouraging readers to ponder the vast implications and abundant possibilities this intersection yields. Through exploration and critical inquiry, we can begin to comprehend not only how AI reshapes creativity but also how it reshapes us.

Chapter 1:
The Dawn of AI in Creativity

As we step into the rapidly evolving landscape of creative industries, the dawn of AI in creativity emerges not as a mere technological advancement, but as a transformative force reshaping the very fabric of art, design, and media. From humble beginnings in academic labs to becoming an integral part of creative workflows, AI has begun to defy the boundaries of human imagination, challenging traditional notions of authorship and aesthetic value. Creative professionals and technology enthusiasts alike find themselves at the crossroads of innovation and tradition, where algorithms and machines offer new possibilities that were once confined to science fiction. This chapter explores how AI is more than just a tool; it represents a dynamic partnership between human ingenuity and machine intelligence, promising to inspire a new era of boundless creativity while urging us to question and redefine our understanding of artistic identity and expression in this brave new world.

Defining Creative Intelligence

In the rapidly evolving landscape of technology, the term "creative intelligence" captures the fusion of artificial intelligence's computational power with the nuanced world of human creativity. This emerging concept challenges traditional definitions of creativity, raising questions about what it means to be creative when machines come into play. Creative intelligence is more than just the ability to generate novel ideas; it involves understanding and applying a diverse set of cognitive and emotional processes. As AI systems are endowed with the ability to learn, adapt, and even improvise, the dawn of AI in creativity necessitates a reevaluation of creativity itself.

The integration of AI into creative processes marks a shift from simply using technology as a tool to viewing it as a collaborative partner in the creative endeavor. Historically, creativity has been seen as an exclusively human domain, deeply tied to emotions and the subconscious mind. With AI, however, questions arise about the potential for machines to replicate or even surpass human creativity. Can an algorithm understand the emotional depth in a piece of music, or appreciate the subtlety of a metaphoric expression in writing? The exploration of creative intelligence seeks to answer these questions.

Creative intelligence combines the analytical prowess of machines with elements of human originality and inventiveness. It involves more than pattern recognition and predictive analytics; it taps into the ability to juxtapose unrelated ideas to create something new. AI's role in this space often begins with data analysis—discovering trends and patterns that humans might overlook. Yet, its contribution extends beyond analytics into generative processes, where AI can produce art, music, and writing that evoke genuine emotional responses from audiences.

At the heart of defining creative intelligence lies the ability to mimic the cognitive processes associated with human creativity. This includes abstraction, analogy, and other mechanisms of creative thought that often defy algorithmic representation. The challenge for AI developers is to encode these processes into machine learning systems that can operate autonomously and intuitively, navigating the complex world of human emotions and cultural contexts.

AI's attempts to understand and reproduce human cognition bring up philosophical questions about consciousness and intentionality. While machines are not conscious and don't possess intentions, creative AI blurs these lines by producing outputs that appear intentional and meaningful. This poses ethical and philosophical questions: Are AI creations authentic expressions of creativity, or are they simply the outcome of sophisticated algorithms? Defining creative intelligence involves responsible exploration of AI's potential without overselling its capabilities.

Historically, art was a means of human expression and communication, deeply intertwined with personal and collective identities. With AI's rising role, the boundaries of creative ownership are continually shifting. When a machine generates a painting or composes a symphony, who owns the resultant work? The programmer who wrote the algorithm, the AI system itself, or perhaps no one? These considerations reframe discussions around intellectual property in an age where creative intelligence is increasingly artificial.

The future involves machines equipped with enhanced creative intelligence working alongside humans to expand creative potential. Such symbiotic relationships might inspire bolder innovations as AI provides new perspectives and tools for human artists and creators. However, to fail to address the disparities in access to AI technologies across the globe could limit creativity to those with resources, thus stalling what could otherwise be a universal creative renaissance.

AI creatively complements human capabilities by managing tasks that require large-scale computation and data-driven insights. This collaboration allows human creators to focus on aspects where they excel—intuition, emotional intelligence, and imaginative leaps—which remain challenging for machines to master. As AI systems are refined to understand context and nuance, they might take on more responsibility, leading to increasingly complex creative outputs that blend machine and human inputs seamlessly.

A critical component of creative intelligence lies in understanding cultural nuances, emotional expressions, and symbolic meanings—all of which are areas where AI is still learning to excel. The richness of human creativity is often culturally situated, and for AI to generate authentic art that resonates globally, it must incorporate a diversity of human experiences and knowledge systems.

Looking ahead, the quest to define and enhance creative intelligence draws inspiration from nature and human cognition, mirroring processes that characterize the human brain. AI developers delve into neural networks that mimic the brain's synapses, creating architectures that foster novel associations and insights. These technological advancements suggest a future where creative intelligence could become a standard complement to human creativity across industries.

While the potential is vast, the integration of AI into creative fields demands ethical considerations. The impersonality of machines creates challenges in ensuring that AI applications uphold human-centric values and contribute positively to society. Navigating these challenges requires continued dialogue between artists, technologists, ethicists, and the public to guide the ethical development of creative intelligence.

In conclusion, defining creative intelligence offers a glimpse into the evolving dynamic between humans and machines. As AI continues to push creative boundaries, it challenges traditional perspectives on creativity and collaboration. By embracing this new paradigm, creators and technologists have the opportunity to shape a future where artificial and human creativity don't just coexist, but thrive together, unlocking possibilities yet to be imagined.

Historical Context of AI in Art

The journey of artificial intelligence in the realm of art is a tale of technological curiosity meeting boundless creativity. The roots of this fascinating intersection stretch back further than one might initially think. While modern advancements have thrust AI into the spotlight, the seeds were sown in the mid-20th century, a time when computer science itself was in its nascent stages. Visionaries like Alan Turing began pondering the potential of machines, sparking questions about their capabilities that would ripple through time.

In the early days, artists and scientists shared a common ground - the desire to explore new frontiers. This curiosity led to the emergence of what we now recognize as generative art. During the 1960s and 1970s, a handful of pioneering artists began experimenting with algorithms and computers, using these tools to generate novel visual forms. Notably, artists like Harold Cohen with his infamous program "AARON" embodied this experimentation spirit. AARON was an early autonomous drawing program, programmed to create artworks that evolved with minimal human intervention.

Given the limitations of technology during that era, the artworks produced were understandably simple compared to today's standards. Still, they represented a critical turning point. These early experiments were not just about creating art; they were philosophical explorations into the nature of creativity itself. They questioned what it means to create and what roles machines could play in this ancient human endeavor.

As we moved into the 1980s and 1990s, the personal computer revolution changed the game. Computers became more accessible, and a growing number of artists began to explore their creative potential. Software development exploded during these decades, leading to an unprecedented intersection between digital technology and traditional artistic practices. Innovators in this period forged new paths, experimenting with digital manipulation and computer graphics, which laid the groundwork for more sophisticated AI applications in art.

During these formative years, the discourse around AI and art was heavily centered on questions of authorship and originality. Could a machine truly be an artist? Or were these computer-generated designs mere extensions of their human programmers? These debates fueled both fear and fascination, pushing the boundaries of traditional art communities and challenging preconceived notions about creativity and intelligence.

The turn of the millennium marked another shift in the historical trajectory of AI in art. Advancements in machine learning and the advent of artificial neural networks introduced more complexity and autonomy in digital creations. This technological leap was crucial in allowing machines to begin analyzing and learning from vast datasets, which in turn enhanced their capacity to generate intricate and varied artworks. Programmers and artists alike seized upon these capabilities, exploring how machines could be trained to mimic or even exceed human artistic methods.

As AI systems became more sophisticated, the range of artistic endeavors they influenced began to widen. Beyond visual arts, AI started making strides in fields such as music composition, literature, and performance art. Collaborative projects sprung up globally, highlighting AI's uncanny ability to work alongside humans as both a partner and a tool in the creative process. These collaborations generated enthusiasm and skepticism alike, triggering deeper inquiries into the nature of creativity and intelligence.

Reflecting on AI's historic journey in art, what stands out is the consistent push-pull between technology and artistic expression. With each technological stride, artists have adapted, responding with new forms and pathways for expression. While initial skepticism often met these advancements, over time, acceptance grew as AI-integrated works demonstrated not only artistic merit but also captured imaginations worldwide.

AI's history in art is not just a story of technological evolution but also a narrative about shifting cultural perceptions. Throughout its development, AI has challenged artists and audiences alike to reconsider the value of human input versus machine-generated output. This ongoing dialogue has ensured that AI's integration into the arts is not just a technical endeavor but a deeply philosophical one.

Looking back, it's clear that the historical journey of AI in art is as much about transformation as it is about continuity. It's a case study in how new technologies can disrupt yet simultaneously preserve artistic identities, drawing upon age-old impulses to innovate and express. As we stand on the precipice of even more dramatic technological breakthroughs, understanding this historical context helps us appreciate the layered, evolving landscape of AI in art, while opening up new dialogues about future possibilities.

Chapter 2:
Algorithms and Artistry

The fusion of algorithms and artistry marks a pioneering shift in how we perceive creative expression, blending the precision of code with the boundless imagination of human creativity. As AI technologies evolve, they unlock fresh pathways for artists and creatives to explore, transcending traditional boundaries of media and technique. Algorithms, once confined to the realm of data processing, now dance with brushstrokes and melodies, enabling machines to emulate, and sometimes surpass, human artistic endeavors. This marriage between machine intelligence and artistic inspiration challenges us to rethink the role of the artist, questioning whether creativity is solely a human domain or if machines can possess a semblance of artistic soul. In today's rapidly changing landscape, artists and technologists alike are compelled to embrace this transformative synergy, harnessing the power of AI to push the frontiers of what art can be, while still navigating the ethical and cultural dimensions that arise. The interaction between pixels and pigments, notes and nodes, not only propels art into novel dimensions but also redefines artistry in an age where algorithms don't just compute—they create.

How Robots Are Learning to Paint

The notion of robots learning to paint might once have sounded like science fiction, but today's technology is increasingly blurring the lines between human and machine creativity. This intersection of algorithms and artistry isn't just transforming how art is made; it's redefining what creativity means in the digital age.

At the heart of robot painting lies machine learning, a technique that allows computers to recognize patterns and make decisions based on data. While the idea of teaching machines to paint may seem like a novel curiosity, it goes far deeper, probing questions about the nature of creativity. What does it mean for a machine, devoid of conscious intent, to create something that humans perceive as art? How do we measure its value and impact when the process is driven by algorithms rather than emotions?

To appreciate how robots are learning to paint, one must first understand the technological components that make this possible. Neural networks, which mimic the human brain's architecture, play a pivotal role. They enable machines to learn from vast sets of data and generate images that mirror the complexity and nuance of human-created art. Each iteration of machine learning models adds new layers of sophistication, developing an uncanny ability to replicate artistic styles, be it the delicate brushstrokes of Impressionism or the structured landscapes of Cubism.

Consider the process of style transfer, a cutting-edge technique where robots take a new image and redraw it in the style of a renowned artist like Van Gogh or Picasso. Through deep learning, machines analyze the intricacies of an artist's method and apply this knowledge to new, yet unseen canvases. This results in a fusion—a vivid exploration between the machine's computation and the organic unpredictability of human creativity.

Despite these marvels, the process isn't without challenges. Machines don't "see" art as we do; they interpret it as a combination of numbers and vectors. Their abilities to replicate existing art forms prompt debates on originality and authenticity. Can a creation born from calculated precision possess the same aura and meaning as one born from human hand and heart? This leads us to reassess the value assigned to art when it's born of silicon rather than instinct.

These endeavors also push the boundaries of collaboration. Artists now find themselves in unique partnerships with technology, working alongside algorithms to explore territory that wouldn't be imaginable alone. The artist becomes a curator of digital imagination, guiding the machine's unsolicited suggestions and blending them with human emotions and ideas. This relationship is symbiotic, where technology enhances but doesn't overshadow human ingenuity.

On a more philosophical level, robots learning to paint stirs conversations about consciousness and creativity's essence. Are these creations simply sophisticated reproductions of neural processes, or do they constitute something fundamentally new—a revolution in artistic expression? Such questions echo historical doubts present in any era of technological progress, reminding us that the tension between innovation and tradition has always been a catalyst for creativity.

Moreover, the accessibility of algorithmic tools democratizes art in a way that was previously unimaginable. They allow a broader population to partake in the artistic process, regardless of formal training or expertise. Platforms that teach machines to paint promise new forms of cultural expression, reflecting a diverse spectrum of perspectives and stories otherwise unheard.

The implications also extend to educational realms, where the next generation of artists grows up influenced by code and canvas alike. They face an exciting frontier, equipped not only with conventional tools but also with the algorithmic prowess to reimagine what it means to create. This merging of traditional skills with digital fluency heralds a fertile ground for uncharted forms of visual communication.

The potential reach of robotic painting isn't limited to the confines of galleries or ateliers. It's poised to influence animation, advertising, and media production, where visual imagination can be augmented by the automation of painstaking artistic tasks. As industries evolve, professionals will need to adapt, finding ways to leverage these tools while preserving the human touch that infuses art with soul.

We stand on the precipice of a new era, where machines aren't just mimicking the masters but are becoming creators in their own right. As this journey unfolds, it provokes us to reconsider long-held ideas about art, expression, and identity. The dialogue between human and machine isn't merely about the abilities of artificial creators but an exploration of our creative boundaries.

In conclusion, the tale of robots learning to paint isn't merely a narrative about technological advancement; it's an invitation. It invites us to engage with a future where creativity knows no single genesis. As we navigate this landscape, the true artistry lies not solely in the finished work but in the collaborative dance—a stunning tapestry woven from the threads of machine potential and the essence of human passion.

AI Composers: Music Beyond Human Imagination

In the realm of creative endeavors, music has always occupied a special space. It's a language that transcends borders and cultures, an expression of human emotion that has been cherished and revered for centuries. But what happens when this deeply personal art form meets the cold, calculated power of artificial intelligence? Can machines, driven purely by algorithms, capture the soulfulness that defines great music? These questions guide us into the fascinating world of AI composers where technical prowess merges with artistry, crafting music that challenges our perceptions of creativity.

The concept of AI-generated music isn't entirely new, but recent advancements have thrust it into the limelight. A multitude of sophisticated algorithms now enable machines to create symphonies and melodies that once seemed exclusive to human virtuosos. At the heart of this revolution are neural networks, particularly deep learning models. These models, inspired by human brain structures, learn and generate music through vast datasets, analyzing patterns, styles, and structures from a wide array of musical genres. The results can be hauntingly beautiful or intriguingly unconventional, subtly bending rules that humans have internalized over millennia.

One of the greatest appeals of AI composers is their ability to explore realms of music that human minds might never touch. They can weave genres together in a blend that defies traditional classification, a mix of classical harmonies with electronic beats, or jazz improvisations with folk themes. This synthesis isn't bound by human limitations like fatigue or bias, driving innovation and offering new perspectives to musicians and audiences alike. While some may argue that these creations lack the nuanced soul of a human-composed piece, others find beauty in the fresh, untainted compositions that arise from sheer computational creativity.

The advent of AI in music composition presents both opportunities and challenges for artists. On the one hand, it serves as a powerful tool for musicians, composers, and producers, enabling rapid prototyping and experimentation. Artists can explore vast musical landscapes without being anchored by technical constraints. Tools like AIVA and OpenAI's MuseNet are democratizing music creation, providing access to compositional resources for novices and seasoned professionals alike. They allow artists to focus more on narrative and emotive content, using AI as a collaborator to flesh out their visions.

On the other hand, questions about the originality and authenticity of AI-generated music loom large. When a machine-driven composition garners acclaim, who holds the artistic credit? Is it the programmer who designed the algorithm, the machine that executed the task, or the musician who curated the final piece?

These are not merely philosophical inquiries but possess significant implications for the music industry's economy and infrastructure. As AI continues to blur the lines between creator and tool, industry and culture are forced to re-evaluate traditional notions of intellectual property and authorship.

Moreover, the emotional enigma of AI-generated music remains a topic of endless debate. Can machines truly imbue their music with emotion, or is it merely a reflection of the data they're trained on? Music elicits a deeply human response, tapping into emotions such as joy, sadness, and nostalgia. While AI can statistically mimic these features, it's uncertain if the same depth of feeling can be achieved without human empathy and experience. Nonetheless, listeners often respond to the emotional triggers embedded in AI compositions, suggesting a subjective experience influenced by individual interpretation more than the music's genesis.

The journey of AI composers also offers a lens into the broader societal and cultural shifts driven by technological innovation. These musical AI systems are a testament to human ingenuity and our insatiable desire to push the boundaries of what's feasible. The convergence of music and AI reflects a significant paradigm shift in how creativity and technology intersect in our everyday lives. As we delve deeper into integrating AI with human-led creativity, it's crucial to consider the cultural resonance, ethical dimensions, and future implications of these hybrid creations.

In an industry-driven by innovation, AI is redefining the landscape of music production and consumption. Even as AI composers create music that astounds and provokes, the human element remains essential. The future of music lies not in replacing human musicians but in augmenting their capabilities, providing tools that extend their creative horizons. Artists who embrace this synergy can venture into new artistic domains, exploring dimensions of sound and harmony previously undiscoverable. This harmonious collaboration between human and machine heralds a new era in the musical narrative, crafting a future where creativity knows no bounds.

Chapter 3:
Design in the Digital Age

As we delve deeper into the digital age, the landscape of design is undergoing a profound transformation, driven largely by the integration of artificial intelligence. This evolution is not just about automating tasks but reimagining the very nature of creativity and innovation in design. AI is introducing a new paradigm, enabling designers to break away from conventional boundaries and explore uncharted territories of aesthetics and functionality. Through complex algorithms and machine learning, AI tools offer unprecedented opportunities to tailor and personalize the design process, making it both more efficient and infinitely more creative. The digital brush strokes painted by AI extend far beyond traditional methods, fostering a collaborative environment that enhances human ingenuity. In this burgeoning era, the synergy between man and machine is not merely supplementary but a catalyst for the next wave of design ingenuity, challenging us to rethink what's possible in our creative endeavors and inspiring a new generation of designers to embrace the potential of technology.

Automating Creativity in Graphic Design

In the age of digital transformation, the role of graphic designers has undergone a seismic shift. Automation, powered by artificial intelligence, is firmly entrenched in this evolution, offering a new toolkit for designers and redefining the creative process. AI's impact on graphic design is not about replacing creativity but enhancing and expanding it, allowing designers to push boundaries in ways once deemed unimaginable.

AI's integration into graphic design starts with the automation of tedious tasks, freeing up time for what many value most—the creative spark. From automatic image tagging to complex photo manipulation, AI tools have streamlined operations that were once time-consuming. AI can swiftly analyze and sort thousands of images, reducing hours of labor to mere seconds. This efficiency not only boosts productivity but also liberates designers to focus on innovative aspects of their creations.

One of AI's remarkable capabilities is its ability to generate new design ideas. Algorithms, trained on a staggering variety of styles and trends, can propose several design options tailored to specific requirements. These tools harness complex layers of data analysis, learning from past designs to craft novel outcomes. By suggesting layouts, color schemes, and font combinations, AI acts as a creative partner, complementing the designer's vision and sometimes uncovering patterns that might have been overlooked.

Despite this, AI doesn't strip away the human element. The relationship between AI and human designers is akin to an artist and their brush; the tool enhances the ability to bring ideas to life. AI's capacity to automate aspects of creativity allows humans to focus on more conceptual tasks, which remain distinctly human capabilities—interpretation, emotion, and cultural relevance. In a way, automation frees creatives to exercise deeper imaginative thinking and experimentation by handling routine chores.

Consider the personalization of content—an area where AI has made a significant impact. Algorithms can tailor designs to fit specific demographics, adjusting to preferences, seasons, and even cultural events. This level of customization enables a more engaging user experience, as products and advertisements are dynamically altered to resonate deeply with target audiences. By analyzing trends, AI ensures that designs are not only relevant but also primed for consumer adaptation.

Moreover, AI's role in graphic design has fostered a more inclusive and diverse landscape. Language and cultural barriers are bridged through AI's language processing capabilities, allowing for seamless global collaboration. Designers can now effortlessly integrate global perspectives into their work, enriching the cultural tapestry of their output. This broadens the horizons of what is possible within the design sphere, creating a melting pot of influences and styles.

The ethical implications of AI in graphic design cannot be ignored. As AI tools become ubiquitous, questions arise about authorship and originality. Is the final creation the product of the human hand or the machine's algorithm? While AI's role is to assist, designers must navigate the fine line between inspiration and replication, ensuring ethical standards and originality are upheld. The conversation around these issues is critical to the future of AI-driven design.

AI's automation in graphic design stretches into realms of accessibility. Tools now assist designers in creating content that is more inclusive, considering visual impairments or cognitive disabilities. With AI, designers can simulate how those with disabilities may perceive their work, adjusting elements to ensure broader accessibility. This approach supports a more equitable user experience, demonstrating that automation can serve both the designer and society at large.

Additionally, sustainability in design benefits from AI. With eco-friendly design practices gaining traction, AI aids in optimizing design resources, minimizing waste, and conserving energy. By predicting and reducing excess material usage, AI ensures design processes align more closely with sustainable goals. This reflects a commitment not just to innovation, but also to responsible stewardship of resources.

Ultimately, automating creativity in graphic design is an evolving journey as AI continually improves. For some, AI represents an augmentation of human potential, while others view it as a tool to democratize creativity. As AI becomes more sophisticated, it challenges preconceived boundaries of design, urging professionals to redefine what it means to create. It's an exciting era where technology and human ingenuity converge, sparking new forms of artistic expression.

This transformative period calls on designers to embrace technology with an open mind. The convergence of AI and creativity in graphic design holds unparalleled potential, inviting a reimagining of the craft itself. How designers choose to leverage these advancements will shape the future of the field. It's crucial to remain adaptable, curious, and critically engaged with these tools to fully realize their potential.

As we move forward, the dialogue between AI and human creativity continues to evolve. This partnership nurtures an environment where creativity knows no bounds, catalyzing an endless array of possibilities. The future beckons a collaborative dance between man and machine, one that promises to reshape the world of design in ways we are only beginning to comprehend.

The Role of AI in Fashion Innovation

In the bustling intersection of technology and creativity, fashion stands as one of the most vibrant canvases where AI's brushstrokes are vividly transforming the landscape. The synergy between artificial intelligence and fashion innovation is not just a recent fad but a profound shift that's reshaping the narrative, design process, and even the future of the fashion industry. As the world becomes more digital, fashion naturally follows suit, embracing AI to push beyond traditional boundaries, offering not just creativity, but also personalization and efficiency.

The AI Muse

AI's role in fashion begins with its capacity for pattern recognition. This ability allows designers to find inspiration in the vast archives of fabric, color, and style that AI systems can analyze in seconds, a task that would take humans hours, if not days. The capacity to identify trends, foresee future styles, and tailor designs that fit individual tastes has revolutionized the design process itself. AI acts as both a digital assistant and a wellspring of ideas, empowering designers to explore realms that were previously unattainable. No longer confined to manual sketching, the modern designer can now unfurl their creative visions through digital simulations, courtesy of machine learning algorithms.

The personalization AI offers can't be understated. In an age where individuality is celebrated, consumers are looking for more than off-the-rack solutions. They want garments that speak directly to their personal stories and unique identities. Here, AI steps in to deliver custom-fit clothing suggestions. By learning from individual preferences and body metrics, AI creates a seamless and intuitive shopping experience. The result is a bespoke selection of recommendations that resonate on a deeply personal level, bridging the gap between what consumers desire and what they purchase.

Beyond design and personalization, AI also streamlines the logistical aspects of fashion. With large-scale production and supply chain complexities, errors can creep in and costs can spiral. AI-driven predictive analytics help brands foresee demand, manage inventory with precision, and even automate the restocking process. This foresight reduces waste, aligns production more closely with consumer demand, and ultimately contributes to more sustainable practices.

Moreover, AI is fostering a more inclusive fashion industry. Virtual try-ons have become a game-changer, allowing customers of all sizes to visualize how garments will look and fit, reducing the shortcomings of static size guides. This technology bridges geographical divides as well, making fashion more accessible to people in remote areas who may not have immediate access to physical stores.

AI has even threaded its way into the creative fabric of fashion through generative design. Designers collaborate with AI to create new patterns, styles, and combinations previously unimagined. By acting as co-creators, AI enables bold and innovative designs, often mingling elements across cultures and eras to craft something fresh and exhilarating. This collaboration opens up avenues for pioneering aesthetics and high-fashion trends.

The rise of AI in fashion also poses new ethical inquiries. As machines take on creative roles, questions around authorship and intellectual property become more pressing. Who gets the credit for an AI-generated design? The lines between human and machine contributions blur, urging the industry to consider new frameworks for creative ownership.

The challenge lies in maintaining the intrinsic artistic touch that fashion demands. Balancing automation with human intuition is crucial. AI tools should not replace the unique sensibilities and emotional insights of human designers but should augment them, freeing them from mundane tasks and allowing them to focus on higher-order creative processes.

Despite the hurdles, the inspirational potential of AI in fashion is inescapable. It invites a reimagining of what fashion can be, pushing it into a realm where technology not only enhances creativity but becomes a partner in pioneering design. For creative professionals, industry leaders, and technology enthusiasts alike, the message is clear: AI is reshaping the industry's landscape, offering possibilities that are only limited by the imagination.

As AI continues to weave its influence across the threads of fashion, it beckons a future where innovation and tradition intertwine, resulting in a tapestry that's as forward-thinking as it is rooted in expressive artistry. The fashion industry stands on the brink of an evolution, driven by technological advances and fueled by the infinite possibilities that AI presents.

Chapter 4:
Storytelling with Machines

As we delve deeper into the realm of AI-driven narratives, it's remarkable how machines are transforming storytelling into a collaborative symphony between humans and technology. This evolution breaks traditional boundaries, offering a canvas where generative algorithms craft narratives that capture human emotion while introducing new dimensions of creativity. The fusion of AI in crafting scripts and producing films has opened doors to previously unimaginable storytelling experiences, where plots unroll with a blend of prediction and surprise. While some fear the machine's encroachment on an inherently human domain, others see it as a transformative partner helping elevate storytelling through data-rich insights that anticipate audiences' desires. By augmenting creative potential, AI challenges us to rethink narrative structures and expands the universe of storytelling in media. This synthesis of creativity and computation not only inspires today's creators but also invites a future where the stories we tell echo beyond the confines of our imagination.

Generative Texts and AI Authors

In the realm of storytelling, where human emotion and innate narrative flair once reigned supreme, a new force has arrived. Generative texts powered by AI are reshaping how stories are crafted, interpreted, and experienced. At the intersection of technology and creativity, AI authors are becoming the unlikely architects of a revolutionary chapter in the creative industries. But what exactly does it mean for a machine to create stories? This question beckons us deeper into the tapestry of digital storytelling, where the threads of logic and creativity are woven by algorithms and neural networks.

The essence of storytelling is in its capability to communicate complex ideas, emotions, and experiences. Traditionally, this was a realm exclusive to human creativity. However, with the advancement of AI, machines have begun to take the pen, or rather the keyboard, writing their own narratives. Leveraging vast datasets and sophisticated language models, AI can generate texts that range from poetry to scripts, each crafted with an unsettling degree of nuance and coherence.

A tale produced by a machine lacks the experiences of a human author. Instead, it harnesses the collective memory stored in billions of individual stories. This reservoir, drawn from books, articles, and every corner of the internet, shapes the backbone of AI's narrative capabilities. By understanding sentence structures, thematic elements, and stylistic tendencies, AI can generate narratives that mirror human creativity on the surface, though speaking from a vastly different origin.

The ability of AI to create coherent and engaging texts poses intriguing questions about authorship. If a machine can produce a novel that captivates audiences, who do we credit as the author? The developer of the algorithm, the machine itself, or the database of human knowledge it draws from? These questions probe deep into our understanding of creativity and originality, demanding a reevaluation of what it means to create.

Generative AI models, such as OpenAI's GPT and others, operate by predicting the next word in a sequence, crafting sentences, paragraphs, and ultimately entire narratives that can appear remarkably human-like. By tweaking inputs and parameters, these models can simulate different writing styles, genres, and perspectives. This ability not only opens a world of creative possibilities but also a frontier of ethical and philosophical dilemmas.

While some view AI authors as tools for democratizing creativity—offering everyone the ability to craft stories, poems, or essays—others see the rise of AI-generated texts as a threat to human craftsmanship. The charm of human-written stories lies in their imperfections and emotional depth, characteristics AI strives to mimic but can never truly replicate. Yet, in an age where speed and volume often override quality, the demand for AI-generated texts may only increase.

This technological upheaval propagates a double-edged promise—on one side, AI authors provide an unprecedented capability to generate content at scale, potentially alleviating creative block or extending creativity into areas previously uncharted by human thought. On the other side, it could saturate the market with content lacking in human warmth and originality, challenging established norms of creative attribution and value.

Interestingly, AI-generated texts are also having a surprising impact on human authors. Collaborating with AI, writers can explore radical new directions, using the machine's perspective to spark ideas they might never envisage. Through this collaboration, humans remain at the helm, steering the narrative while machines tirelessly explore the vast possibilities of language. This represents a new form of creative symbiosis, where the boundaries between human and machine creativity become increasingly blurred.

The key to harnessing AI in storytelling lies in its partnership with human creativity. By combining the precision and consistency of algorithms with the empathy and intuition of human imagination, the potential for innovation is enormous. Writers can use AI to overcome the rigidity of writer's block, experiment with styles unseen in human art, or even simulate dialogues and worlds with a degree of detail unattainable solo.

Moreover, the integration of AI into storytelling does not only signal the emergence of new types of content but also the transformation of how audiences interact with stories. Personalized narratives that adapt to readers' preferences or even real-time story generation are becoming feasible, portending a future where stories are as dynamic as their readers.

Perhaps the magic of storytelling doesn't reside in the uniqueness of its creator but in its ability to evoke emotion and imagination in a reader. As AI authors continue to evolve, they may redefine the pathways of emotional resonance and the very nature of narrative engagement. By becoming both co-creators and competitors, AI authors challenge human storytellers to push beyond traditional storytelling paradigms, innovating in ways previously thought unimaginable.

In the grand tapestry of creative endeavors, AI narrative generation stands as both an extension and a disruption. It is an extension in that it provides new tools for exploration, allowing us to expand our creative horizons. Simultaneously, it disrupts longstanding notions of authorship and originality, urging creatives to reconsider the essence of their art.

As we advance, the narrative of AI authors will continue evolving, emboldened by technological progress and societal adaptation. It's critical that we examine this evolution with an eye towards both opportunity and caution. By understanding and guiding the development of generative texts, we can ensure that this transformative force in storytelling enriches our creative landscape, respecting the integrity of human imagination while exploring the boundless potential of machine creativity. In doing so, we embrace a future where stories are not merely told, but experienced in myriad unprecedented forms.

AI in Film and Media Production

As we delve into the exploration of AI's integration into film and media production, it's clear that these technologies are not just tools but collaborative partners reshaping the boundaries of creativity. The evolution of filmmaking has always been intertwined with technological advancements, whether it's the transition from silent movies to talkies or the advent of computer-generated imagery (CGI). Now, AI stands on the cusp of ushering in another revolutionary era.

AI in film and media is largely centered around three core areas: scriptwriting, editing, and animation. These are disciplines where AI's ability to process vast amounts of data and recognize patterns can yield unprecedented creative possibilities. In scriptwriting, AI algorithms can analyze thousands of screenplays, distilling the elements of what makes a story compelling. This analysis can aid writers in crafting narratives that resonate on a deeper, more universal level. While AI can offer new narrative structures, the human touch ensures the stories remain imbued with emotion and authenticity.

The editing room is perhaps where AI's impact is most immediately tangible. Traditional film editing is a meticulous process, requiring editors to sift through hours of footage to craft a coherent and impactful story. AI can revolutionize this by using machine learning algorithms to identify patterns and suggest edits. In documentaries, for instance, AI can help comb through archival footage, recognizing key themes and suggesting narrative constructs. This ability not only speeds up the editing process but allows for more complex and layered storytelling.

When it comes to animation, AI is breaking down barriers that have long been considered insurmountable. With deep learning techniques, AI can automate the rendering of complex animations, reducing what used to take months into mere weeks or even days. Companies are utilizing AI for tasks like motion capture and character rigging, which traditionally required hours of laborious effort. This shift enables artists to focus more on the creative and conceptual aspects rather than the technical execution.

Consider the film "The Irishman," where AI played a crucial role in de-aging the actors. This was not simply a matter of applying digital prosthetics but involved sophisticated machine learning techniques that analyzed the actors' earlier filmographies, learning their facial expressions and body language across time. Techniques like these demonstrate AI's ability to bring new life to storytelling, constantly pushing creative boundaries and redefining the 'possible' in cinematic ventures.

Moreover, AI is revolutionizing the realm of virtual production. By integrating AI with real-time rendering and LED screens, filmmakers can create immersive environments without ever leaving the studio. This is particularly beneficial in light of global challenges like the COVID-19 pandemic, where traditional location shooting has become more difficult. Virtual production empowered by AI enables films to maintain high-quality visuals while ensuring safety and flexibility.

It's also worth noting AI's significant role in media accessibility. By generating subtitles and dubbing with near-perfect accuracy across various languages, AI can help expand a film's reach without compromising the creator's original vision. These advancements also create a more inclusive cinematic experience, enabling a diverse audience to enjoy and engage with content.

However, these technological advancements brought by AI come with a set of ethical and practical challenges. The ownership of AI-generated creative content remains a complex issue. Could an AI ever be credited as a co-author of a screenplay it has helped shape? This poses profound questions about ownership, rights, and collaboration in the creative industry. Furthermore, there's the risk of homogenizing creativity—if too many films start using similar AI-generated solutions, audiences might perceive these works as formulaic.

Furthermore, AI's fast pace in film production necessitates a reevaluation of traditional roles within the industry. As AI takes on more roles in script analysis, editing, and even directing, creatives must evolve in their roles, leveraging AI to enhance, rather than replace, the human artistry at the heart of film. This requires a shift in skills, where understanding AI's capabilities and constraints becomes essential for the modern filmmaker.

Despite these challenges, the potential for AI in film and media production is immense. Leveraging AI can lead to an era of personalized filmmaking, where stories can be tailored to individual viewer preferences, creating personalized content experiences. This adaptation not only changes how we consume media but also impacts how stories are told, demanding deeper engagement and connection between creators and their audiences.

Looking forward, the next step involves intertwining AI with augmented and virtual reality technologies to realize truly interactive and immersive storytelling. AI can analyze viewers' reactions in real-time, adapting narratives to match the emotional journey of each audience member. This interaction blurs the lines between viewer and participant, offering fresh potential for storytelling innovation.

In the grand tapestry of creativity, AI is both the brush and the hand guiding it. It remains a tool shaped and wielded by human imagination, imbuing stories with complexity and diversity like never before. As the partnership between humans and machines grows more sophisticated, it opens windows to worlds yet unexplored in the film and media landscape, inviting new stories and storytellers to rise.

The voyage into this brave new world is still unfolding, promising a future where storytelling is a vivid testament to human and machine synergy, an uncharted narrative yet to be written.

Chapter 5:
The New Aesthetic Paradigm

As AI continues to weave its way into the creative fabric, we're witnessing an unprecedented shift in aesthetics, pushing boundaries beyond traditional art forms. This new aesthetic paradigm, courtesy of machines once relegated to mundane tasks, challenges us to rethink the essence of creativity. By infusing logic with limitless permutations, AI allows artists and designers to explore dimensions that were previously unreachable. It's not just about creating new art; it's about redefining our relationship with creativity itself, making room for hybrid forms that merge human intuition with machine precision. This evolution is not merely the introduction of novel tools but a radical transformation of envisioning art's purpose and potential. As we navigate this uncharted territory, the potential for innovation grows boundless, urging us to redefine artistic value and stretch the limits of our imagination. This chapter sets the stage to dive deeper into how these emerging technologies cultivate entirely new expressions of art, forever altering the aesthetic landscape and challenging the way we perceive beauty and artistry in the modern world.

Emerging Art Forms Enabled by AI

We're standing at the threshold of a new artistic era, one where artificial intelligence not only participates in the creative process but also initiates its own forms of expression. AI's influence stretches beyond traditional artistic techniques, cultivating novel mediums and methods of creating art. These emergent forms, often described as blends of technology and imagination, challenge the very definition of art itself.

Take, for instance, the generative algorithms that paint. These algorithms don't merely replicate human brushstrokes; they invent unique styles and compositions. As AI models evolve, they've begun to escape the confines of their initial programming to develop original art forms. This phenomenon suggests that AI isn't just an assistant in art; it's an autonomous creator, conjuring pieces previously unimaginable.

Let's consider "neural network art," a prime example of AI-driven innovation. In these works, neural networks learn from a dataset of images to create new visual experiences that captivate audiences not just with their aesthetic appeal, but with their conceptual depth. Artists employing these techniques can ask: What does it mean to create art in partnership with a machine that learns and evolves?

The advent of AI poetry has opened new frontiers in literary creation. By harnessing large language models, poets are crafting verses that tread the line between human sentiment and machine logic. These poetic works, woven with words suggested by AI, explore complex emotional landscapes and redefine what can be perceived as beautiful or meaningful. In essence, AI can become both a muse and a medium.

Similarly, in music, AI has been transforming soundscapes. Musicians are now collaborating with AI systems to produce compositions that defy traditional boundaries, blending genres and incorporating sonics outside the realm of human creativity. The result is a new, co-evolved musical genre that celebrates the convergence of machine precision and human emotion.

In the realm of sculpture and physical art, 3D printing dovetails with AI to produce intricate designs previously thought impossible. AI models optimize structures for both aesthetics and functionality, creating objects that are as beautiful as they are efficient. These are art pieces born from algorithms, bridging the gap between digital conception and tangible creation.

Virtual reality (VR), augmented reality (AR), and AI intersect to create immersive experiences that alter our perception of the world. These technologies invite audiences to step into digital landscapes where the line between the creator and the observer blurs. Artists using VR and AR powered by AI offer viewers not only a chance to observe art but to inhabit it.

Installations have also seen a transformative shift. Interactive artworks powered by AI engage spectators like never before, leveraging real-time data and machine learning to create responsive environments. These installations adapt to their audience, making each experience unique, personalized, and dynamic.

There's a growing community of artists interested in exploring AI's role in ecological art. They use AI to interpret environmental data, transforming this information into compelling art pieces that heighten awareness of ecological issues. In this way, art does not merely depict nature—it becomes an integral part of the discourse on the environment.

AI also plays a significant role in art restoration and conservation. Sophisticated algorithms can now analyze centuries-old paintings and sculptures, offering insights into their original form and optimal methods for preservation. This AI-enabled understanding helps extend the life of art for future generations, ensuring the legacy of human creativity endures.

As we venture further into this new realm, AI challenges traditional notions of authorship and creativity. Who gets credit for an AI-generated piece? Is it the programmer, the algorithm, or perhaps even the machine itself? These questions compel us to rethink the established paradigms of originality and ownership in art.

Moreover, the rise of AI in art provokes a reevaluation of artistic value. Does a piece's worth lie solely in human input, or can a machine-produced work hold equivalent value? This ongoing debate has sparked a wider conversation about the nature of creativity and the evolving criteria by which we define art.

Despite these challenges, the potential of AI in art is undeniable. Creative professionals are embracing AI's capabilities, exploring how these technologies can inspire innovation and facilitate new artistic expressions. As AI becomes an ingrained tool in artistic practice, it offers both opportunities and provocations for artists to explore.

In conclusion, AI is not simply a tool in the artist's arsenal but a catalyst for unprecedented creativity. It is an agent of change that pushes the boundaries of artistic intent and execution. By facing the ethical, cultural, and practical implications head-on, we position ourselves at the forefront of a revolution in art.

Amidst these changes, we find ourselves in a space where tradition meets innovation, where machines challenge our perceptions and redefine what it means to be creative. The alliance between humans and AI in art heralds a future rich in possibility, one where the collaboration sparks inspiration that lights the way forward for generations to come.

Machine Creativity and Artistic Value

The artistic landscape is evolving rapidly, with AI at the forefront driving a seismic shift in what we consider creativity. Machine creativity challenges the long-held belief that artistic value originates exclusively from the human mind. As we witness AI crafting intricate paintings, composing symphonies, and scripting evocative narratives, we're beckoned to reassess our understanding of art itself. It's not just about machines doing tasks historically reserved for humans; it's about them doing so in surprisingly innovative ways, forging new paths that were previously unimaginable.

Some may argue that machines lack the consciousness needed for true creativity. However, machine creativity lies in the algorithmic exploration of vast possibilities, generating outputs that can inspire human creation. A painter, for instance, might draw inspiration from an AI-generated image, integrating its abstract elements into their own canvas. This interaction suggests that artistic value doesn't solely hinge on the creator's humanity but perhaps on the impact the work has and its capacity to evoke emotion and thought.

One prominent domain where machine creativity is making waves is in the visual arts. Algorithms process thousands of images to create new composites, producing pieces that expand the boundaries of traditional aesthetics. These creations, borne of computational processes, often resonate with a human audience by invoking the uncanny, the unexpected, or the beautifully abstract. In this space, the machine acts not just as a tool but as an artistic partner, encouraging artists to explore hitherto unexplored aesthetic pathways.

Moreover, AI's influence extends beyond individual creations; it's reshaping entire art forms. By employing neural networks in film production or generative design in architecture, creators can transcend conventional limits. The resulting works challenge perceptions, inviting audiences to experience art not just as passive observers but as active participants engaging with evolving narratives. This dynamic interplay offers new layers of meaning, adding depth to the artistic experience and pushing the boundaries of creativity forward.

This transformative power of machine creativity raises questions regarding artistic authorship and value. If a machine generates a painting that stirs deep emotion, who is the artist? Is it the programmer who designed the algorithm, or the AI that synthesized the art? Or could it be a collective authorship encompassing humans and machines alike? The answers aren't straightforward, yet they are crucial in redefining how we assign value and credit in an increasingly algorithm-driven creative world.

Despite the complexities, there's much to appreciate about machine contributions to the arts. AI systems can generate vast numbers of creative options, empowering artists to choose and refine those that resonate most deeply with them. This partnership offers a new model of co-creation, where artists and machines collaborate to infuse artistic endeavors with a richness that neither could achieve alone.

Interestingly, the democratizing effect of machine creativity can't be overlooked. With AI tools accessible to more people than ever, individuals outside traditional artistic circles are empowered to create and share their work. This proliferation of creative expression dilutes gatekeeping in art and design, allowing a broader spectrum of voices to contribute to cultural dialogues. Artistic value, then, becomes inclusive, embracing diverse perspectives and experiences enhanced by AI's capabilities.

What emerges from this is an expanded definition of creativity. Traditionally, creativity was seen as a mysterious human trait, linked with emotion and inspiration. Now, it's increasingly seen as a process that encompasses technology, networks, and algorithms. This shift compels us to reconsider what makes art "valuable". Could it be novelty, expression, cultural relevance, emotional impact, or perhaps something we can't yet define? The dialogue AI initiates about these questions is vital, encouraging introspection and evolution.

Significantly, artists are leveraging AI to surpass their own limits. Musicians, for instance, use AI to detect patterns in sound, resulting in innovative compositions or completely new music genres. AI augments their creative processes, providing fresh ideas or solving technical challenges. Similarly, writers may find inspiration in AI-generated text, which can nudge them toward creative breakthroughs. The amalgamation of human and machine creativity fosters unprecedented artistic innovation, a testament to the synergy born from this partnership.

Yet, we must be conscious of the risks associated with machine creativity. While AI offers incredible potential, it also poses ethical dilemmas, including issues surrounding copyright, the authenticity of machine-generated works, and potential biases inherent in AI algorithms. Addressing these concerns is essential to ensure that machine creativity enhances the artistic landscape responsibly and inclusively.

In conclusion, the advent of machine creativity invites us all to participate in redefining artistic value. As AI becomes an increasingly co-creative force, it challenges us to think critically about what constitutes art and what we hold dear in its creation. Embracing this dialogue can lead to richer, more nuanced artistic experiences and open pathways for yet-unimagined forms of expression. The convergence of technology and art is here to stay, shaping a vibrant future where human and machine establish a new creative paradigm together.

Chapter 6:
AI and the Evolution of Advertising

In the dynamic world of advertising, AI has emerged as a catalyst for transformation, reshaping the industry with precision that was scarcely imaginable before. By harnessing vast troves of data, AI empowers advertisers to craft campaigns that resonate on a deeply personal level, intriguing audiences with bespoke experiences. This data-driven approach capitalizes on machine learning algorithms to analyze consumer behaviors, preferences, and trends, enabling creatives to design tailored content that speaks directly to individual needs and desires. AI's adeptness at generating insights facilitates not just personalization but also the creation of unparalleled, engaging narratives that captivate consumers' imaginations while maintaining authenticity and relevance. As AI continues to evolve, it beckons industry leaders and creative professionals alike to explore a future where advertising is not just informed by data but inspired by it, guaranteeing that the message reaches not just the audience, but the right audience at precisely the right moment.

Data-Driven Creative Solutions

In the evolving landscape of advertising, AI has become an essential partner, transforming the creative process with a precision that was once unimaginable. The use of data-driven creative solutions has revolutionized how brands connect with their audiences, enabling not only personalized marketing but an entirely new dimension of audience engagement. By analyzing rich datasets, AI unveils insights that drive the creation of compelling, emotionally resonant messages that reach the right people at the right time. This convergence of AI analytics with creative ingenuity marks a dance between data and art, challenging the limits of traditional advertising methods.

AI offers unprecedented access to consumer behavior, preferences, and trends, dissecting information from social media, purchase histories, and even real-time interactions. The ability to process and learn from these massive datasets means that AI can predict consumer desires before they even surface. This predictive power allows advertisers to craft messages that speak directly to the individual, tapping into personalization at a scale previously out of reach. Consider the difference: a static advertisement that shouts to the masses versus a bespoke campaign that whispers directly to each viewer, understanding their unique language of interest and engagement.

Furthermore, the speed at which AI works ensures that creative solutions remain dynamic and responsive to the ever-shifting nature of digital consumerism. In the past, adapting a marketing strategy could take weeks, if not months. Now, AI systems react in real time, adjusting campaigns as they learn, optimizing for better performance even within a campaign's lifespan. This leads to continuous improvement, refining methods based on data feedback loops to enhance effectiveness.

But how does this blend of data and creativity actually take shape? At the heart of it is the AI's ability to generate creative content based on patterns and trends extracted from data. Through machine learning algorithms, AI can craft diverse creative assets – be it visuals, text, or audio – tailored to audience segments identified through data analysis. It's an iterative process where each new layer of data informs the next level of creative output. This results in messaging that feels not just crafted, but crafted for you.

While technology steers the rudder, human creativity remains the wind in the sails. The role of human designers, writers, and strategists becomes one of guiding and refining AI outputs, ensuring that content remains rooted in authenticity and emotional depth. This collaboration can be seen as a symbiosis where AI handles the heavy lifting of computation and data analysis, while humans apply the finesse and nuance that only lived experiences can bring. AI enables, but it's human insight that elevates.

The impact of such solutions extends beyond mere consumer engagement; it also optimizes spending by ensuring resources are directed towards the most effective strategies. Companies no longer rely solely on intuition or educated guesses to allocate their marketing budgets. Instead, data-driven insights lead to more informed decisions, drastically reducing waste and maximizing ROI.

However, integrating data-driven creative solutions isn't without its challenges. Ethical considerations arise concerning data privacy and the responsibility of businesses in handling consumer information. The balance between personalization and privacy must be carefully managed to build and maintain trust. Moreover, the reliance on algorithms raises questions about the retention of human creativity and the risk of homogenized content.

Yet, these challenges also present opportunities. As AI continues to mature, there's an open field for new innovations that prioritize ethical standards while still pushing the boundaries of creativity. The future, then, hinges not just on technological advancements but also on developing frameworks that ensure these tools are used responsibly and with discernment.

It's clear that AI's rise in data-driven creative solutions isn't just transforming advertising – it's redefining it. The partnership between data and creativity has shifted the narrative from mere outreach to meaningful dialogue. Brands are not just telling stories; they're engaging in conversations, meeting consumers where they are and where they aspire to be.

As AI continues to shape the future of advertising, industry leaders and creative professionals find themselves at the brink of endless possibilities. The challenge is to harness this potential, infusing it with innovation and ethical mindfulness. In doing so, the advertising landscape becomes not just a display of creativity, but a testament to human ingenuity enhanced by intelligent machines.

Personalized Marketing Campaigns

The field of advertising has always thrived on the power of personalization. The more precisely a message is tailored to its audience, the greater its impact. Yet this ambition has, until now, been restrained by the practical limits of data analysis and human creativity. Enter AI, a game-changer poised to dismantle these barriers. AI not only processes vast amounts of data swiftly but also discerns patterns and preferences that are often invisible to the human eye. It enables advertisers to craft marketing campaigns so uniquely targeted that they seem almost custom-made for each consumer.

In the era of AI, personalized marketing campaigns have transcended traditional boundaries. Advertisers are no longer reliant solely on demographics. Instead, they harness the nuanced insights AI provides from digital footprints—browsing habits, social media interactions, and even voice assistant queries. This data wealth allows for hyper-personalization, where each consumer is treated as a market of one. This capability isn't just a technological advance; it's a paradigm shift, redefining how brands engage with their audiences.

However, the implications of AI-driven personalization extend beyond the ability to gather and analyze data. At the heart of these AI systems are algorithms designed to learn and adapt continuously. These systems can predict consumer behavior, anticipate needs, and suggest products with an accuracy and timeliness that feels intuitive. Imagine an online shopping experience where recommendations do not merely reflect past purchases but anticipate future desires—transforming browsing into an experience of continual, serendipitous discovery.

Consider the example of chatbots powered by AI, which have revolutionized customer service interactions. These digital assistants are crafted to not only address customer queries but to do so in a manner that feels personal and engaging. By analyzing the language and tone of the consumer's messages, AI can tailor responses that resonate emotionally, further enhancing the sense of personalization. This level of interaction fosters a deeper connection between brands and their customers, driving loyalty and retention.

The role of AI in creating personalized marketing campaigns extends into content creation itself. Machine learning algorithms can generate ad copy and visual content that are optimized for individual tastes. By analyzing engagement metrics, AI can determine what images, colors, or phrases captivate distinct audience segments. This adaptive content strategy ensures that marketing materials don't just reach an audience; they engage it on a profound level.

As AI enables more sophisticated personalization, ethical considerations become paramount. The boundary between beneficial personal insights and intrusive surveillance must be navigated with care. Consumers are becoming more aware of how their data is used, necessitating transparency and ethical stewardship from brands leveraging AI technologies. Businesses must cultivate trust by safeguarding data privacy and ensuring that personalization enhances user experience without overstepping boundaries.

Moreover, the efficiency of AI in targeted advertising campaigns necessitates a thoughtful approach to creativity. While algorithms facilitate personalization by analyzing data at unprecedented scales, the human touch remains vital. Creativity infused with human empathy and understanding continues to play a crucial role in shaping messages that resonate. The ideal synergy lies in combining AI's data prowess with the imagination and emotional depth that only humans can provide.

Looking forward, the landscape of personalized marketing campaigns will become increasingly dynamic. Innovations in AI promise even deeper levels of customization with real-time adjustments and anticipatory marketing strategies that not only respond to consumer actions but also predict them. This evolving capability offers brands the thrilling potential to engage customers in ways that feel authentically personal and profoundly meaningful.

The trailblazers of this AI-driven personalization wave are rewriting the rules of consumer engagement, merging the power of technology with the human elements of creativity and connection. As AI tools evolve, fostering richer and more nuanced communication pathways, they expand the horizon of possibilities for marketers. The marriage of AI and personalized marketing campaigns is only beginning to reveal its transformational potential, heralding a new age where relationships between brands and consumers are more intimate and impactful than ever before.

Chapter 7:
AI Tools for Creatives

In a world where blending pixels and algorithms is rapidly becoming the modern palette and canvas, AI tools for creatives represent a seismic shift in how art is conceived and crafted. Software like neural networks and machine learning algorithms are not just tools; they are collaborators, infusing new life into the imaginative processes across visual arts, music, and design. These AI advancements streamline workflows, allowing creatives to harness vast arrays of possibilities, enabling everything from intricate pattern generation to predictive editing and personalized art pieces. At the heart of this digital renaissance lies the intersection of artificial intelligence and human imagination—a partnership that invites artists to wonder just how far their creative visions can stretch. By augmenting human capacity, AI encourages creatives to dream bigger, transcending traditional boundaries and redefining what is possible in the art world. Through this symbiosis, AI isn't just reshaping creative processes; it's catalyzing a revolution, inspiring artists to explore, innovate, and push the horizons of their crafts like never before.

Software Revolutionizing Artistic Workflows

In the rapidly evolving landscape of art and design, artificial intelligence (AI) is redefining how creatives interact with their tools. The current wave of AI-powered software is not merely auxiliary; it fundamentally reshapes the creative process. Artists and designers are leveraging AI to enhance their workflows, integrating technologies that allow for unprecedented levels of efficiency and innovation. These advancements usher in a new era where practical magic meets the canvas of human imagination.

AI-driven software applications have become integral to artistic workflows by taking over repetitive tasks, thereby enabling artists to focus on higher-level creative decisions. For instance, generative design algorithms offer infinite variations on a single concept, allowing designers to explore a multitude of possibilities with just a few clicks. This not only expedites the design process but also opens up new creative avenues that were previously unfeasible.

A key player in this revolution is machine learning, which equips software to learn from vast amounts of data to produce outputs that echo human creativity, yet transcend conventional limitations. In fashion, AI helps predict trends by analyzing vast datasets, helping designers craft collections that align with consumer desires before they are even articulated. Similarly, in graphic design, AI tools like Adobe's Sensei and Autodesk's Dreamcatcher empower users by automating mundane tasks such as color correction or layout adjustments.

The most compelling aspect of AI in artistic workflows is its ability to foster collaboration between human intuition and machine precision. Tools designed with AI algorithms provide suggestions that spark innovation by offering entirely new perspectives. They allow artists to blend disparate styles and mediums in ways that were near impossible before. The results are often startling, revealing hidden connections and visual languages that redefine our understanding of form and function in art.

These transformative technologies are also democratizing the world of creative arts. With AI-powered tools, artistic creation is more accessible than ever, breaking down barriers that once isolated fine art to those with lengthy apprenticeships or formal education. Novices can now explore complex artistic styles through user-friendly platforms that harness AI capabilities, therefore expanding the creative pool and introducing a diversity of voices previously marginalized by technical gatekeeping.

This democratization does not come without its challenges. AI software requires a delicate balance to maintain unique artistic identities while enhancing productivity. Many artists wonder where the soul of creativity lies when software takes the reins of artistic decisions. However, the fusion of AI into artistic workflows should be considered less as an abdication of control and more as an augmentation of the creative mind. It allows the artist to envisage new artistic realms enriched by technology.

Moreover, AI's impact extends beyond visual arts to music, literature, and beyond. Music composition software, for example, uses AI to generate melodies that compete with those of human composers, enhancing the creative process by reducing the time required for composition. Literary AI tools help authors not only draft but also edit their work, offering stylistic suggestions based on comprehensive analysis of language trends and reader preferences.

Despite the many advantages of AI software in artistic workflows, ethical considerations arise. Concerns over the authenticity of AI-generated art pose real questions about ownership and the definition of creativity. As AI tools become better at mimicking human expression, distinguishing between machine and human-created works becomes a nuanced endeavor. The key is to navigate these concerns with a focus on the potential to elevate rather than undermine human creativity.

Ultimately, the landscape of artistic workflows empowered by AI is still in its nascent stage. Yet, it continues to expand the horizons of what is possible in the creative realm. Coders, technologists, and artists must collaborate continually to refine these tools, ensuring they serve as catalysts rather than barriers to creative growth. By channeling the capabilities of AI, creatives can visualize ideas that push traditional boundaries, paving the way for art that resonates on new emotional and intellectual frequencies.

Through the convergence of art and technology, AI's role in revolutionizing artistic workflows highlights a future where human imagination intertwines effortlessly with machine logic. This collaborative dynamic promises not just an evolution, but a revolution—one where art and AI together create a tapestry of possibilities that inspire a new generation of artists to redefine creativity's limitless potential.

The Intersection of AI and Human Imagination

As we delve into the intersection of AI and human imagination, we're crossing into a fascinating landscape where technology meets the boundless creativity of the human mind. This confluence isn't merely a merging of computational power with artistic vision but a revolution reshaping how ideas are conceived, developed, and brought to life. What was once within the exclusive domain of human creativity now finds a companion in the realm of artificial intelligence, birthing possibilities previously unimagined.

For creatives, AI tools offer new dimensions of inspiration and innovation. AI doesn't just process data; it interprets and generates. It brings to the table an ability to analyze vast datasets, synthesizing information at speeds far beyond human capability. Picture this: an artist inspired by the brushstrokes of countless artists, facilitated through AI's vast repository of art. Here, AI acts as a mentor of sorts, guiding, yet leaving room for the artist's personal touch.

In the creative process, AI can assume roles that complement human endeavors. Consider an AI collaborator that generates multiple variations of an idea, allowing designers to choose paths they might not have considered independently. This AI-generated diversity enriches the creative process, turning it into a symbiotic dance where human intuition and AI precision lead to unexpected revelations.

For instance, in visual art, AI's ability to remix and reinterpret images introduces artists to novel visual styles. This is not a replacement of the traditional form but an extension—expanding the palette of possibilities. AI allows creatives to explore what-if scenarios in their work, pushing them to new horizons and challenging their understanding of art and creativity.

When it comes to music, AI can compose based on existing styles or generate entirely new harmonies and rhythms. It's a fascinating dialogue between the musician and the machine; melodies emerge from algorithms but are imbued with emotion and context by human hands. This process challenges conventional notions of authorship, placing AI as both tool and collaborator.

The reimagining of creative boundaries doesn't stop at individual disciplines. By integrating AI into multidisciplinary projects, creators can broaden their scope even further. Consider a filmmaker using AI to predict audience reactions, adjusting narrative elements to evoke specific emotions. AI not only aids in crafting stories but also personalizes experiences, bringing viewers closer to the narrative like never before.

Yet, amid these technological advances, the core of creation remains unchanged. AI may enhance and expand, but it can't replace the human heart's creative impulse. It is imagination that assigns meaning to form and function, coloring AI's raw, neutral capabilities with purpose and emotion. Creators breathe life into algorithms, imbuing them with narratives that resonate and inspire.

AI-driven tools act as catalysts for creativity, urging us to question and to explore further. They challenge the status quo, urging artists and innovators to rethink what is possible. While it's easy to see AI as an end in itself, it's vital to recognize it as a tool—one that enhances human potential rather than replaces it.

This partnership between AI and creativity also raises profound questions about originality and authenticity. How do we regard art created with AI involvement? What role does the creator play in this collaborative dance? These questions aren't just ethical puzzles—they're defining concepts for what creativity will look like moving forward.

As we stand at the threshold of a new era marked by this intersection of AI and imagination, the creative community must embrace AI not just as a tool but as an ally. It's about fostering a new dialogue—one where we integrate AI's strengths with human nuances. In this way, we not only expand our creative capacities but also redefine the imaginative potential of what it means to create and be human in the 21st century.

Ultimately, the intersection of AI and human imagination opens a dialogue that encourages a blend of the technological with the humanistic, forcing us to ask larger philosophical questions about the nature of creativity itself. It's a dynamic interplay where the impacts ripple through culture and art, prompting profound shifts in how we perceive, create, and engage with the world around us.

While the convergence of AI and creativity is still unfolding, a new narrative is forming. One where AI serves as a bridge, linking the unimaginable with the possible, and helping to craft a shared vision of innovation that embodies both machine efficiency and human depth. This is the dream at the heart of AI's intersection with human creativity—a dream that continues to transform and redefine artistic frontiers.

Chapter 8:
Challenges and Limitations

In our exploration of AI-driven creativity, it's crucial to address the formidable challenges and limitations that accompany these advancements. While AI offers a wealth of possibilities, it also raises significant questions about the nature of authenticity and originality in machine-created art. The essence of human creativity is deeply entwined with personal experience and emotion, elements that machines can't genuinely replicate. This brings us to the delicate act of balancing automation with the irreplaceable human touch in creative processes. Moreover, as AI continues to evolve and integrate into the arts, there's a pressing need to navigate the ethical landscape of AI-generated works. Creative professionals must grapple with the implications of relying too heavily on technologies that might overshadow genuine human talent, potentially homogenizing artistic expression. Navigating these challenges requires a thoughtful approach, embracing the opportunities AI presents while critically examining its impact on the soul of creativity. As we move forward, these issues will increasingly define how AI and creativity coexist, demanding both caution and courage from innovators and artists alike.

Authenticity and Originality in Machine-Created Art

Amidst the swirling wave of technological advancement, AI's entrance into the creative sphere stirs a profound debate about authenticity and originality in art. These aren't just buzzwords nestled within high-brow art critiques but represent the meandering essence of what it means to be genuinely creative in an ever-evolving digital landscape. Imagine a computer generating a painting – does it carry the same essence or "soul," if you will, as one created by human hands? The challenge lies in how we perceive originality and authenticity in art birthed from the cold calculus of algorithms.

Authenticity, as traditionally understood, involves a reflection of the creator's intent, emotions, and personal expression. Human art is evocative, rich with history, context, and the idiosyncratic nature of its creator. Machine-created art, however, challenges this notion by introducing a new kind of neutrality – and with it, an intellectual question: Does the absence of human influence preclude authenticity? The answer, layered and nuanced, invites both skepticism and intrigue.

For starters, machines don't possess consciousness, which makes their creations devoid of personal narrative or emotional depth. This lack of subjectivity raises questions about the originality of AI output. Is the art created by machines truly novel, or is it merely a reconfiguration of existing data? AI's ability to remix, reinvent, and reimagine previously established patterns often produces works that echo familiar themes, thereby testing the boundaries of originality. Even if an AI-generated piece appears unique, its roots inevitably trace back to datasets groomed by human input.

Moreover, the intriguing element of AI-generated art is its dependence on the human creator behind the algorithm. The true originator is often the person programming the machine, imbuing it with specific styles, preferences, and data. They serve as digital curators and editors, guiding AI in its creative ventures. Thus, the authenticity of these works derives partly from the human touch that calibrates the algorithm's creativity, insinuating at least a partial human authorship underlying the machine's mimicry.

Some argue that AI art's authenticity lies in its process rather than its outcome. The procedural novelty – the idea of a non-human entity crafting something aesthetically or conceptually novel – provides a different dimension of authenticity. This penchant for a process-focused authenticity reframes the conversation, offering a fresh perspective that celebrates not only the product but the innovation behind it.

In our quest for understanding AI in art, it's important to realize that machine-created pieces need not compete directly with human art for validation. Instead, they carve out a distinct niche, challenging us to redefine authenticity and originality in art. As we unravel these concepts, we're prompted to rethink our initial, often rigid, definitions of creativity.

Artists, technologists, and audiences alike are inclined to explore coexistence rather than dichotomy in AI-generated creativity. By challenging conventional categorizations, we aren't simply accepting machine art as authentic but are expanding our understanding of what authenticity can entail. This expansion fosters a broader narrative, one that includes but isn't confined to, human emotion and intention.

Notwithstanding, this disruption doesn't come without complications. The blending of human and machine creation also poses ethical considerations that deserve our attention. Who is credited as the original artist – the machine, the programmer, or the collaborative conglomeration of both? Issues of authorship and copyright become entwined in a complex legal and moral tapestry, echoing broader discussions being explored about AI's role in society.

The rise of AI in art compels us to confront these challenges while offering a unique opportunity for analytics and introspection. By pushing the boundaries of tradition, AI art reflects our societal shifts, embodying the tensions and triumphs of merging technology with the intimate act of creation. Through this lens, even the controversy surrounding AI art enriches its dialogue about originality and authenticity.

As we trek further into this digital era, the conversation about authenticity in machine-created art won't be resolved in a singular narrative. Instead, it will evolve, much like art itself, continually influenced by cultural contexts and technological strides. Each AI-crafted artwork forces us to revisit and rethink what art can be, expanding the horizons of creativity beyond the human imagination.

Thus, AI doesn't diminish human artistry but instead offers new tools and paradigms to expand the scope of what art entails. By accepting the complexities of these challenges, we open ourselves to an enriched creative dialogue, advocating for an inclusive artistic arena where human and machine creations coalesce. We are invited to reimagine the parameters of art, acknowledging AI's potential to transcend its limitations and inspire a new era of originality, even within the framework of machine generation. The journey into AI-driven art, with all its nuances, might ultimately redefine what it means to be creative, crafting a future where art knows no boundaries beyond our own evolving perceptions of authenticity.

Balancing Automation with Human Touch

In the fast-paced world of AI in creative domains, the quest to balance automation with the human touch presents both a challenge and an opportunity. As AI continues to evolve, its capabilities in generating art, music, and design push the boundaries of what machines can create. But can it truly replicate the essence of human creativity, characterized by emotional depth, intuition, and uniqueness? This question doesn't have a straightforward answer and deserves careful examination and reflection.

Automation offers unprecedented efficiency, enabling creative professionals to execute tasks with precision and speed previously unimaginable. From automated design tools creating templates in seconds to AI algorithms composing music that mimics the style of renowned human composers, the potential productivity gains are staggering. However, in embracing such efficiencies, there's a risk of losing the nuances that human creativity imparts. The essence of art often lies not in its flawless execution but in its imperfection, a quality that's inherently human.

The delineation between mechanized efficiency and human artistry becomes blurred when AI is involved in creative processes. AI-enabled tools have become adept at identifying patterns, styles, and even emotional cues in a set of creative works. Yet, the outcomes often lack the deeply personalized and subjective experiences that humans bring to their creative endeavors. Artistic expression is not merely about aesthetic achievement but also about conveying personal experiences and cultural narratives.

In many creative industries, the challenge is how to maintain these human elements while leveraging automation's benefits. For example, in graphic design, AI can generate multiple design iterations in minutes, allowing designers to focus their energies on more complex and meaningful aspects of creative projects. Designers can then inject their distinct perspectives and experiences into this process, ensuring that creativity remains deeply human-centric despite technological advances.

One approach to ensuring that automation contributes meaningfully to creative processes without overshadowing the human element is through thoughtful integration and collaboration. By viewing AI as a partner in creativity rather than a replacement, creatives can harness its power to enhance rather than dilute their vision. This partnership allows for the mundane tasks of creation to be managed by machines, freeing human creators to explore beyond the basic constructs of their art forms and reach new creative heights.

There are profound concerns about relying too heavily on AI within creative contexts. Creativity is, at its heart, a subjective experience rooted in human consciousness. AI systems, however sophisticated, do not possess consciousness or emotions. They analyze existing data meticulously but lack true understanding. As a result, the art created by machines can feel hollow or derivative, unlikely to move audiences in the same way as works born from human dreams and struggles.

Moreover, when art is reduced to a reproducible formula, it risks becoming predictable and stale. What makes an artwork evocative often lies beyond mere technique—it's in emotional resonance, the unspoken conversation between the artist and observer. Automation lacks this intuitive understanding and spontaneity, which imbues human work with its spirit and vitality.

There's also an inherent danger in letting machines make creative decisions independently. Artists are individuals shaped by a multitude of experiences—cultural, historical, personal—that no machine can replicate or fully comprehend. By relying too heavily on automation, there's a risk of homogenization, where diversity and innovation give way to machine-driven conformity. To balance this, creatives must ensure that their unique identities guide the use of AI in their work.

As AI technologies continue to integrate into artistic practices, the education of creatives becomes crucial. Fostering an understanding of AI tools and their applications should go hand in hand with encouraging traditional artistic skills and intuition. Bridging this gap necessitates a new kind of artistry, one that embraces technology as a means of extending creative possibilities while holding fast to the human core.

Ultimately, the heart of the matter lies in reimagining the relationship between humans and machines. The potential of AI in art is not about replicating or replacing human creativity but about expanding its reach. By thoughtfully incorporating AI into their toolkits, artists and creators can explore unforeseen possibilities, blending calculative precision with emotive storytelling. This coalescence of machine-generated art and human oversight is where the magic will unfold.

Navigating the intricate dance between automation and the human touch requires introspection, adaptability, and vision. It's less about choosing one over the other and more about finding synergy in their coexistence. As AI continues to redefine the creative landscape, the challenge will be to ensure that art remains an authentic expression of human experience—a testament to our innate desire to create, communicate, and connect.

Chapter 9:
Ethical Implications of AI in Art

The intersection of artificial intelligence and art introduces a complex tapestry of ethical questions that challenge traditional notions of creativity and authorship. As AI systems evolve into sophisticated creators, they blur the lines of copyright and ownership, raising important questions about who truly owns the final product. Are these works owned by the developers of the AI, the users who input the data, or do they merely exist in a liminal space of autonomous creation? Moreover, the implications stretch beyond legal constructs to the moral realm, where the autonomy of machines to create independently invites a reconsideration of artistic intent and integrity. If AI can autonomously produce works previously conceived as uniquely human, we must ask ourselves about the ethical boundaries of machine-generated art. Are we diminishing the value of human involvement, or are we expanding the very definition of art? These questions press upon us the need to establish ethical frameworks that not only protect intellectual property but also embrace a future where technology and human creativity coalesce, forging new pathways in art that challenge conventional boundaries while invigorating the potential for innovative expression.

Copyright and Ownership in AI Creations

The intersection of artificial intelligence and artistic creation has introduced unprecedented questions about copyright and ownership, stirring debates that challenge traditional norms and legal frameworks. Historically, the concept of authorship has been predicated on the notion of a human creator, one who exercises intellectual and creative control over their work. However, with AI increasingly involved in generating art, music, literature, and more, the conventional boundaries of authorship are blurring, prompting a reevaluation of what it means to "own" a creative piece generated by machines.

At the heart of this discussion lies the fundamental question: who, or what, is the rightful owner of AI-generated content? Is it the developer who created the algorithm, the entity that generated the input data, or possibly the AI itself? Each of these perspectives presents its own ethical implications. Currently, copyright law doesn't recognize AI as a legal entity capable of holding ownership; thus, the rights typically fall to the human agents behind the AI—be they programmers, users, or collaborators. But as AI continues to evolve in its creative capabilities, this interpretation might prove insufficient for future considerations.

The involvement of AI in creative processes spans a broad spectrum. On one end, there's the AI acting as a tool, an extension of the artist's brush or the writer's pen. Here, the human retains control over the creative vision, using AI merely to execute or explore their ideas. In these cases, the ownership seems more straightforward: the human creator holds the copyright. However, on the opposite end of the spectrum, AI operates autonomously, generating content with minimal human intervention beyond initial programming settings or datasets. This raises the question of whether the traditional views on authorship can be sustained when AI contributes significantly to the creative process.

In recent judicial developments, courts have started to address these issues. For instance, there have been cases where algorithms created intricate works of art, leaving courts to determine whether the resulting pieces were eligible for copyright protection and, if so, who held that copyright. The rulings have varied, often leaning toward the protection of human creators but highlighting the legal system's struggle to keep pace with technological advancements. Nevertheless, these legal challenges underscore the pressing need for a reimagined framework that accommodates the unique nature of AI's contributions.

Creative professionals and industry leaders are at the forefront of navigating this intricate landscape. For many, AI presents an opportunity to augment their crafts, allowing them to push creative boundaries and explore unchartered territories of expression. Yet, the question of ownership remains a crucial consideration, as the determination of rights affects distribution, credit, and economic benefits. The industry must grapple with these issues to ensure that innovation and artistic exploration are not stifled by outdated legal interpretations.

As debates about AI authorship percolate, there's an impetus for collaboration between technologists, artists, and legal experts to redefine copyright laws. A nuanced approach might involve a tiered ownership model that affirms the rights of all human contributors involved in shaping the AI's output. Such a model could acknowledge the complexities of co-creation while still preserving the incentive structures necessary for innovation and creativity. Additionally, there could be systems that recognize the unique contributions of AI without conferring personhood, thus sidestepping the thorny legal implications of recognizing machines as rights-bearing entities.

Beyond legal parameters, the philosophical questions of AI's role in creativity are equally absorbing. If AI can produce works indistinguishable from human-created art, does it alter the perceived value or authenticity of the piece? Should society view AI not just as a tool but as a collaborator in artistic processes? These questions extend beyond ownership rights, prompting a broader contemplation of how creativity is defined in an era increasingly marked by technological hybridization.

The cultural implications of AI-created works also provoke a necessary dialogue about the source of artistic inspiration and the nature of creativity itself. AI tools, drawing on vast datasets, might produce works that reflect diverse cultural inputs, effectively democratizing art by blending global influences. Yet, they might also perpetuate the biases embedded within those datasets, leading to ethical concerns that must be critically addressed by the creative community.

An exploration into the copyright and ownership of AI creations is not just a legal exercise—it's an invitation to reexamine the very foundations of creativity. By engaging with this subject, technology enthusiasts and creative professionals can foster a more inclusive, understanding art world. This world embraces both human and machine contributions, leading to richer, more diverse artistic expressions.

To preserve this cultural richness and ensure fair distribution of rights, stakeholder dialogues must continue to evolve. It is essential for creative sectors to collaborate across disciplines, championing regulatory innovations that reflect AI's growing role in the arts. As they push creative boundaries, they must also shape an ethical framework that respects the complexity and nuance intrinsic to AI-generated art. Such efforts will enable communities to embrace not only the technological possibilities but also the moral and philosophical considerations that accompany them.

The Moral Dilemmas of Autonomous Creativity

The advent of AI in the creative process poses significant moral dilemmas that challenge traditional notions of authorship, ownership, and responsibility. As machines generate art, music, and literature, the question of "who creates" looms large. AI, seemingly devoid of consciousness, creates in ways that mimic human intuition and spontaneity, leading us to a crossroads where the lines between human and machine creativity blur.

A primary concern is the concept of agency. When a machine produces an artwork, who is the artist? Does the programmer who created the AI system hold the creative credit, or is it the machine, which operates with a degree of autonomy? Traditional copyright laws struggle to address these nuances, leaving creators and regulators in uncharted territory.

Moreover, the role of intentionality in art creation becomes a contentious issue. Human artists imbue their work with emotions, experiences, and intentions—a tapestry of conscious thought woven into the creative fabric. Can AI, which lacks self-awareness, truly possess intention? Or is its creativity a mere reflection of the data it processes?

Art has long been a mirror of the human condition, an expression of our innermost thoughts and societal paradigms. Autonomous AI creativity tests this notion, generating art that is oftentimes indistinguishable from human-created works but devoid of lived experience. This raises philosophical questions about the essence of art and its connection to human identity.

Furthermore, considering ethical standards and accountability for AI-generated work presents its own set of dilemmas. If an AI produces content viewed as offensive or damaging, who bears responsibility? Is it the company that developed the AI, the user who deployed it, or the algorithm itself? These questions underline the need for clear guidelines and ethical frameworks that address accountability without stifling innovation.

One cannot ignore the impact on the human workforce. As AI takes on more creative roles, will human artists be rendered obsolete? There's a genuine concern that machines could displace artists, leading to an erosion of creative professions and the rich diversity of human expression that comes with them. On the flip side, AI can act as a catalyst, empowering creatives to explore uncharted territories and extend their artistic capabilities.

Simultaneously, there's the potential for a democratization of art. AI tools can provide access to creative expression for individuals without traditional artistic skills or means, leveling the playing field. This shift could lead to a renaissance of creativity, diverse in perspectives and abundant in innovation.

The ambiguity surrounding an AI's moral compass is another significant concern. Humans imbue their creations with ethical and moral values, often guided by cultural and personal norms. An AI, without innate understanding, relies solely on algorithms and data input, potentially perpetuating biases inherent in its training data. This mechanized worldview can result in creative outputs that clash with human ethical standards or overlook complex societal issues.

Autonomous creativity also brings forth the discussion on the intrinsic value of art. If AI can create dazzling symphonies or paintings without human intervention, does it trivialize the labor and emotion humans invest in art? Or does it invite us to redefine our appreciation, viewing art as a dialogue between human intent and machine capability?

The potential for AI creativity to evolve in ways we cannot yet imagine is vast. It opens doors to new art forms and mediums that challenge our perceptions of creativity itself. This ongoing evolution begs for a reevaluation of traditional ethical frameworks, encouraging a shift towards a model that embraces both innovation and moral accountability.

In navigating these moral dilemmas, stakeholders—artists, technologists, ethicists, and policy makers—must engage in open dialogues. Collaborative efforts can ensure AI's role in the creative process respects human values, reflects diverse societies, and fosters a future where human and machine creativity coalesce to enrich our world. Embracing AI's potential while considering its ethical implications can lead to a harmonious synthesis of old and new, human and machine.

Chapter 10:
Cultural Shifts in the Creative Landscape

As artificial intelligence increasingly integrates into the realm of creativity, it's catalyzing profound cultural shifts across the artistic landscape. AI isn't just a tool—it's becoming a transformative force challenging traditional concepts of artistic identity and redefining global art movements. While some fear the erosion of human touch, others see an opportunity to push boundaries and explore uncharted territories that expand our definitions of art itself. This intersection of technology and creativity invites artists, designers, and innovators to not only embrace new mediums but also to contemplate the evolving narratives of human expression molded by machine influences. By fostering diversity and inclusivity through AI-mediated practices, we're witnessing a vibrant democratization of creativity, where the lines between creator and creation blur into possibilities once thought unimaginable. In this shifting terrain, the creative community must navigate these cultural currents, crafting a future where technology enhances rather than diminishes the human spirit's innate artistry.

AI's Influence on Global Art Movements

The influence of AI on global art movements marks a fascinating intersection where technology meets creativity. In recent years, as AI technology develops at an unprecedented pace, it's reshaping how artists across the globe create, share, and interpret art. This infusion of AI into the art world isn't just a fleeting trend but a powerful catalyst for change, expanding the boundaries of what's possible in artistic expression.

Historically, art movements have often emerged in response to societal changes, technological advancements, and cultural shifts. The Renaissance, for instance, was driven by the rediscovery of classical philosophies and advances in technique. Similarly, AI now fosters a new wave of artistic transformation. From AI-generated paintings and installations to novel musical compositions, the scope of this digital renaissance is immense. These works, which sometimes challenge the fundamental definitions of "art" and "creator," are rapidly becoming embedded in the global cultural fabric.

In Asia, the influence of AI in art is vividly evident. Artists in Japan and South Korea are pioneers in integrating AI into visual and performing arts, embracing technologies that enhance traditional art forms. South Korean artist Shinseungback Kimyonghun, for instance, uses AI algorithms to blend photography and digital manipulation, creating pieces that question human identity in a digital age. This kind of innovative engagement doesn't just produce remarkable art but also facilitates a dialogue about the influence of technology on human existence.

Europe has long been the cradle of artistic evolution, and its current embrace of AI is no exception. In cities like Berlin and Paris, the convergence of artists and technologists has birthed a new breed of AI-inspired art collectives such as Obvious and artist Mario Klingemann, who explore the limits of machine creativity through generative adversarial networks (GANs). This collaboration not only generates stunning artworks but also places AI-generated art in public consciousness, engaging audiences in discussions about the nature of creativity itself.

The Americas, particularly North America, are at the forefront of AI-driven art experiments. The United States, with its Silicon Valley-led tech-centric mentality, has seen several groundbreaking AI art projects supported by research institutions and tech giants. Artists like Refik Anadol, who transforms data into hypnotic installations, use AI to question the complexity of human environments and digital landscapes. In Latin America, collectives are using AI to address socio-political themes, illustrating AI's potential to reflect and amplify the region's unique artistic voice.

Africa, often overlooked in tech conversations, is emerging as a hub for AI innovation in art. Artists are harnessing AI tools to document and reinterpret traditional cultural narratives, blending them with modern digital aesthetics. Initiatives like the Arts in Africa Collaborates Lab are indicative of the continent's efforts to include AI in creative dialogues, facilitating art that speaks to both contemporary and ancestral African experiences.

Artists in the Middle East, too, are utilizing AI to address themes of identity, tradition, and modernity. The region's art scene, rich in history and cultural depth, sees AI as a means to interpret and reimagine historical narratives. Through AI, they're exploring new dimensions of ancient art forms while engaging with contemporary issues, thus fostering a unique synthesis of the old and new.

These global movements reveal AI as a universal language, transcending geographic and cultural boundaries. Yet, the implications go beyond the artworks themselves; they extend into the realms of cultural identity and artistic freedom. AI raises pressing questions about authorship, the nature of creative labor, and what it means to be a creator. As AI routines take on more roles traditionally held by human artists, cultural establishments world over are faced with reevaluating criteria for artistic merit and the essence of creativity.

Moreover, the advent of AI art movements prompts a critical reflection on the cultural monopolization of technology. With AI tools primarily developed in tech-heavy regions, there's a conversation to be had about access and equity in artistic innovation. The democratization of AI in art could open pathways for underrepresented voices, enabling a more inclusive global art ecosystem.

In tandem with these developments, AI-driven art keeps pace with or even precedes social changes. It serves as both a mirror and a catalyst, reflecting current societal conditions and propelling cultural dialogues. The cultural shifts facilitated by AI in the art world challenge institutions and audiences alike to reconsider and widen their definitions of art.

Undoubtedly, AI's influence on global art movements urges us to consider the ethics and responsibilities inherent in this technological age. As we embrace these new tools, the onus is on us—artists, technologists, and cultural leaders—to leverage AI not just for novelty, but for fostering a better understanding of human creativity and identity. The potential of AI in art is vast and yet to be fully explored, holding promises for enriching our global cultural landscape in previously unimaginable ways.

Redefining Artistic Identity

As AI technologies continue to infiltrate the creative landscape, they introduce possibilities that challenge and reshape the very essence of what it means to be an artist. This intersection of technology and creativity urges a re-examination of artistic identity, paving the way for new paradigms where human and machine creativity converge to produce novel forms of expression.

For centuries, the identity of an artist has been deeply intertwined with notions of originality, personal vision, and the mastery of skills honed over years of practice. The arrival of AI disrupts these qualifications, prompting us to ask: Can a machine possess artistic identity? And if so, does it undermine or enhance the human's role in creative processes? These questions demand exploration as we navigate this evolving terrain.

AI, with its relentless capacity for learning and mimicry, poses a unique challenge to our traditional understandings of creativity. Unlike human artists, AI doesn't require sleep, emotional input, or rest, allowing it to tirelessly generate works that can mimic and surpass conventional norms. Yet, while AI can replicate human styles and even innovate beyond, it's essential to acknowledge that these creations are deeply rooted in historical data fed into the algorithms by humans.

In this intricate dance between human intention and machine execution, we find the seeds of a new artistic identity—a hybridity that defies the need for human art to remain solitary. AI amplifies the potential for collaboration, offering creators a uniquely powerful partner. Many artists are learning to see AI not as a threat, but as a co-creator, reshaping the canvas, page, or screen in ways previously unimaginable.

For instance, visual artists today utilize AI-driven tools to explore vast permutations and nuances in color, form, and composition, leading to works that reflect a fusion of human concepts and algorithmic innovation. Musicians are increasingly experimenting with AI to compose symphonies and songs, introducing melodies and harmonies that stretch the boundaries of auditory experience beyond the confines of human capability.

Yet, this redefinition doesn't imply the erasure of human artistic identity. Rather, it prompts a reevaluation of what it means to be original in an era where AI can assist in crafting complex pieces of art. This new age doesn't render human creativity obsolete; instead, it enlarges the canvas, allowing artists to explore territories that were once out of reach, thanks to technological augmentation.

In redefining artistic identity, a key factor involves reconsidering the role of intention in art creation. Traditionally, intention and emotion have been seen as inherently human traits. However, as AI becomes more integral to artistic processes, the dynamics of intention become complex. Who holds the intention in a piece created by AI? Is it the programmer, the artist using the tool, or the AI itself through its interpretation of patterns and datasets?

This ambiguity also reflects in how we value art. Historically, the value of art is often tied to the artist's identity, their life story, struggles, and triumphs channeled into creative works. With AI, the narrative shifts from the notion of a solitary genius to one of collaboration and systems-based creation, expanding our definitions of what is valuable and why.

One might ask if AI art can stir the same emotions as those created by humans. The answer lies not wholly in the output but in the dialogue it inspires. Art by AI engages us differently—it is an invitation to ponder, to question the nature of creativity itself. The artist, now a part of a larger synergy with technology, cultivates new forms of engagement and new realms of critical discourse.

Moreover, the rise of AI in creativity challenges conventional understandings of authorship and ownership. With technology as a partner, questions arise about who ultimately owns a creation—an aspect that has significant ethical and legal implications within artistic communities. While this matter extends beyond identity, it is undoubtedly entwined with how artists view themselves within this new ecosystem.

Engaging with AI, artists may find their roles transformed from creators to curators or conductors, guiding AI to sculpt ideas set by creative visions. This relationship echoes symbiosis rather than competition, where the artistic process becomes a reflection of collaboration between human cognition and machine processing.

The redefinition of artistic identity is also a cultural dialogue. As AI permeates different art forms globally, it doesn't just impact individual artists but also entire cultures' artistic expressions and identities. The fusion of AI with culture-driven creativity can lead to a renaissance of novel styles, previously unseen, intertwining diverse cultural narratives with technological advancement.

Ultimately, this era of AI-enhanced creativity inspires us to lift our gazes from the limitations of what has been done and cast our sights toward what can be achieved when human and AI intellects interlace. The transformation isn't in the tools themselves but in the minds willing to embrace the flux, challenge conventions, and redefine the boundaries of what art can be.

In conclusion, as AI continues to redefine artistic identity, our focus pivots from the undying fear of replacement to an inspired embrace of evolution. This transformation involves recognizing art as a living, breathing entity, constantly reshaped by our tools and our imaginations. The potential lies in our ability to navigate these changes with grace and insight, crafting a future where artistic identity is not just preserved but vivified and enriched.

Chapter 11:
Human-Machine Collaboration

The collaboration between humans and machines is reshaping the creative landscape, marking a transformative chapter in the history of art and design. At the heart of this development is the profound partnership that has emerged, allowing creators to harness AI's computational prowess to enhance their artistic visions. This chapter explores how this synergy is blurring the lines between creator and tool, enabling a dialogue where human intuition meets machine logic. In this dynamic interplay, AI serves not just as a passive instrument but as an active collaborator that expands the boundaries of creativity itself. With algorithms accelerating the exploration of novel forms and concepts, artists and designers are engaging in co-creation processes that challenge traditional notions of authorship and originality. As we delve into these new partnerships, we will see that the essence of creativity is not lost but rather evolving, opening up boundless possibilities and inspiring a reimagined future for art and technology alike.

Co-Creating with AI: A New Partnership

As we delve deeper into the digital age, a fascinating collaboration between humans and artificial intelligence (AI) emerges. This partnership is not merely transactional but has the potential to redefine creativity itself. As AI becomes more sophisticated, it's crucial to recognize how these technologies augment human potential, opening new frontiers in art, design, and media.

In the past, artists and creators were often lone figures, crafting their works through sheer skill and imagination. Now, they're teaming up with algorithms and machine learning tools to push creative boundaries. This collaboration raises questions: What does it mean to create with machines? How does this partnership shape our understanding of creativity? We find answers in the innovative ways these collaborations manifest.

One prime example is the realm of visual arts, where AI can generate complex patterns and images that inspire artists to explore new styles. Rather than replacing the artist, AI serves as a catalyst, provoking ideas and enabling creators to break away from traditional constraints. This symbiotic relationship offers a profound rethinking of art creation processes, where AI acts as both a tool and a collaborator.

Consider the use of generative algorithms in design. These algorithms can analyze vast datasets and generate unique design solutions that human minds might never conceive on their own. Designers can harness these computational capabilities to iterate quickly, develop novel aesthetics, and solve complex problems. This partnership allows for a convergence where creativity becomes more exploratory and less deterministic.

The music industry is another area where AI's influence is felt strongly. By analyzing patterns in notes, rhythms, and melodies, AI synthesizes fresh compositions, often collaborating with musicians to create unprecedented sounds. Here, AI listens and learns, becoming a partner in the creative process. Musicians leverage these capabilities, incorporating AI-generated elements into their compositions, leading to music that resonates with a modern audience captivated by innovation.

The potential of AI in storytelling is equally transformative. With AI, writers experiment with narrative structures and character developments in ways that traditional methods could not accommodate. AI can suggest plot twists and character arcs, offering an endless supply of narrative possibilities. The collaboration doesn't replace the writer's voice; instead, it complements it, sparking creative ideas that enrich the storytelling experience.

Moreover, AI tools in filmmaking can enhance visual effects and streamline production processes, allowing filmmakers to realize their visions with greater precision and efficiency. By doing so, AI not only democratizes access to complex visual effects but also challenges filmmakers to rethink standard practices, often leading to innovative cinematographic techniques and narrative approaches.

This co-creation extends to fashion and industrial design, where AI assists in developing designs that merge aesthetic appeal with functionality. By analyzing materials, consumer preferences, and global trends, AI helps designers create products that are not only beautiful but also attuned to practical demands. This partnership ensures that design evolution is attuned to both aesthetic qualities and consumer needs.

Despite these advantages, the human-AI partnership is not without its challenges. Issues of authorship and originality arise when machines significantly contribute to creative outputs. Can a work largely created with AI be genuinely considered an original piece? While these questions remain unresolved, they fuel a critical discourse about the essence of creativity and the role humans play in this co-creative process.

The cultural implications of this partnership are vast. By working with AI, creators reflect on what it means to be human in a world where machines play increasingly vital roles in our lives. This collaboration is a testament to human resilience and adaptability, proving that creativity knows no bounds when we open ourselves to new tools and possibilities.

To fully embrace this co-creation, industry leaders, artists, and technologists must collaborate conscientiously. They need to ensure ethical use of AI by recognizing potential biases in datasets and promoting transparency in its creative applications. As AI becomes more ingrained in creative industries, these considerations are essential steps in building a future where humans and machines create in harmony.

Ultimately, this new partnership between AI and humans marks a pivotal moment in the evolution of creativity. It challenges us to rethink our roles as creators and embrace the unknown. As AI continues to transform our industries, it becomes not just an external force but an integral partner in our creative journey.

Blurring the Lines between Creator and Tool

In the evolving landscape of human-machine collaboration, the distinction between creator and tool becomes increasingly nebulous. The boundary that once defined the artist as the sole arbiter of creation is now blending with the capabilities of artificial intelligence. The role of AI in the creative process challenges our understanding of authorship and creativity itself, raising questions about what it means to be a creator.

As AI tools become more sophisticated, they function less like passive instruments and more like active partners in the artistic process. Consider how AI algorithms can now generate entire compositions across various art forms, from music to visual art. It's no longer a simple transaction where a tool executes a human's command. Instead, the tool is part of a dynamic interplay that can influence the direction of the project. This partnership between human creativity and machine intelligence opens up unprecedented possibilities for innovation.

One might wonder if this change diminishes human creativity, but in truth, it often enhances it. By outsourcing certain tasks to AI, creatives free themselves to explore more complex and abstract ideas, focusing on the conceptual and emotive aspects of their work. For example, an artist might utilize an AI to generate a series of patterns or melodies that they can then modify and adapt, injecting their unique style and perspective.

Moreover, AI's capacity to analyze massive datasets provides creatives with insights that might have been impossible to glean on their own. By identifying trends and patterns, AI can help inform an artist's choices, directing their focus toward elements that resonate with current or predicted cultural movements. This ability to sift through and distill information transforms AI into an invaluable collaborator in the design and execution stages.

While AI's utility in the creative process is undeniable, it also raises profound questions about authorship. When a machine contributes significantly to an artwork, who can claim ownership? The artist who conceived the idea, or the AI that helped bring it to fruition? This blurred ownership complicates traditional notions of authorship and calls for a reexamination of intellectual property rights in the age of AI.

Furthermore, as AI models are trained on existing works, they blend numerous influences into new creations. This mosaic-like approach can sometimes lead to unexpected, but stunningly original, outcomes that neither the human nor the machine could predict independently. This unpredictability is at the heart of the excitement and anxiety surrounding AI in the arts: it democratizes access to creativity but also challenges conventional hierarchies of talent and expertise.

The collaborative nature of AI tools prompts us to redefine creativity itself. Traditional definitions that hinge on originality and intentionality must expand to accommodate hybrid forms of creation. These new models recognize the fluid interchanges between technology and artistry, acknowledging that inspiration can be a shared process rather than a solo endeavor.

Perhaps the most profound implication of AI's role as both creator and tool is how it alters our perception of value in art. While some critics argue that art generated by algorithms lacks a soul, others see it as a valid evolution of artistic expression, one that can evoke emotions and prompt reflection just as powerfully as human-made art. The discourse around AI as a creative entity is not merely about technology but about the essence of what we value in creative works.

Despite these advances, human oversight and interaction remain crucial. Machines, for all their capabilities, lack the emotional intuition and ethical compass that guide human artists. This necessitates a symbiotic relationship where AI acts as an extension of the artist's capabilities, augmenting rather than replacing human skills. Collaborations between humans and machines encourage artists to think beyond conventional boundaries, pushing them to explore new territories that might have remained inaccessible without technological intervention.

As we adapt to this new reality, it's essential to cultivate a culture of experimentation and openness. Encouraging artists to embrace AI tools without fear of losing their voice or integrity requires education and dialogue. By framing AI as a co-creator, we can inspire a generation of artists ready to pioneer this frontier, equipped with both traditional skills and technological literacy.

The unity between human and machine creativity signifies a transformative era in artistic expression, one where the lines between creator and tool continue to blur. By embracing the potential of AI, creatives can transcend traditional limitations, ushering in a new chapter of innovation that celebrates diversity, collaboration, and the limitless possibilities of human imagination intertwined with artificial intelligence.

Chapter 12:
Inspiring Innovation

In an era where the creative process is continuously being revolutionized, AI stands poised as a powerful ally to inspire innovation beyond our current imagination. By infusing traditional creative routines with computational intellect, we're witnessing the dawn of unprecedented creative boundaries being pushed and redefined. This symbiotic relationship between humans and machines has shifted how we generate ideas, allowing for a dynamic exploration of concepts that were once confined to the realms of fiction. The role of AI transcends mere tool usage, enhancing ideation processes and offering endless canvases for creative minds to paint their visions upon. As we continue to explore these frontiers, the potential to redefine artistic paradigms becomes not just a possibility but an exhilarating inevitability, spurring a renaissance of creativity that bridges technology with the intangible aspects of artistic originality. Ultimately, this chapter aims to illuminate the transformative journey of creativity through AI, challenging innovators to embrace this new partnership and explore its profound possibilities.

Pushing Creative Boundaries with AI

History has shown us that every technological leap propels creativity into new realms. AI, with its cognitive capabilities and learning algorithms, invites us to explore uncharted territories where the traditional confines of creativity dissolve. This transformation is not mere conjecture; it's reshaping how art, design, and media intersect with human imagination.

Consider the notion of creativity itself. For centuries, creativity was seen as an exclusively human trait, something that machines—with their binary logic—could not emulate. However, AI has started to challenge that perspective by offering a new palette of tools and methodologies that expand creative horizons. These tools not only enhance the efficiency of creative processes but open doors to possibilities previously unimaginable.

A novel artwork no longer relies solely on human intuition. Artists now collaborate with neural networks, setting parameters for machines to generate visuals and audio that can surprise even the artists themselves. It's not a mere imitation of human creativity but an augmentation, turning mere ideas into tangible innovations. The polyphonic potential of AI encourages creatives to push further, experimenting with form, style, and medium.

Yet, the relationship between AI and creativity raises compelling questions. Can a machine truly 'create' art? Or does it simply mimic and iterate existing data patterns? The answer lies in the dynamic between human ingenuity and machine learning. AI serves as a critical catalyst, offering new depths and dimensions to artistic exploration. Thus, it dares artists to challenge traditional notions and redefine what it means to be creative in a digital age.

One striking example of AI pushing boundaries is its influence on design thinking. Graphic designers are leveraging AI for generative design, where machine learning algorithms propose myriad solutions to a single problem. These options expand the designer's toolkit, allowing for more refined and unique outcomes. Fashion designers use AI to predict trends, automate fabric creation, and personalize fashion experiences, ensuring each creation carries the weight of informed creativity.

In media production, AI algorithms edit footage, enhance audio quality, and even script narratives, making production processes more efficient. The intricate interplay of AI and human creativity in film and television offers entirely new genres of storytelling that challenge audiences to ponder the essence of narrative and its delivery.

Of course, the conversation about AI's role in pushing creative boundaries wouldn't be complete without acknowledging the ethical intricacies that accompany it. As AI takes on more creative tasks, stakeholders—artists, technologists, and audiences—are tasked with navigating questions of authorship, authenticity, and ethical use. These considerations are not barriers but rather gateways to deepening our understanding of creativity's scope and definition in the modern world.

Just as the boundaries of AI's capacities are only beginning to be realized, so too are the limits of human creativity being extended. By embracing AI as a creative partner rather than a competitor, creators can explore avenues that are beyond the reach of either entities alone. The coalescence of AI's analytical power and human emotion-driven creativity can foster unexpected innovations, transforming problems into opportunities and ideas into visionary projections.

There's also an inspiring egalitarian promise in AI's influence on creativity. Artists from diverse backgrounds and with differing levels of access to traditional resources are empowered by AI's democratizing potential. With AI, the barriers to entry for creating meaningful art are reduced, allowing new voices to emerge on platforms that were previously inaccessible.

However, leaning into this frontier requires us to continuously question and learn from AI's integration into creative processes. As AI continues to evolve, so must our understanding and adaptation to ensure this powerful relationship reaches its fullest potential. Those in the creative industries must foster a continuous dialogue between human creativity and AI capabilities, learning to balance collaboration with cultural sensitivity and ethical responsibility.

Ultimately, AI's role in pushing creative boundaries offers a glimpse into a future where creativity is reimagined and redefined. It beckons a paradigm shift, challenging us to look beyond conventional frameworks and embrace a future where machines and humans jointly curate the creative experience. As we move forward, our collective ability to adapt, inspire, and innovate will set the standard for how art, in any form, is perceived and appreciated.

The age of AI is one of promise and potential. While the challenges are many and complex, with unwavering curiosity and stewardship, we can ensure that AI remains a tool for expanding, rather than limiting, the creative frontier. Through this partnership, we have the opportunity to not only push the boundaries but also to redraw them, creating art that speaks to the shared imagination of human and machine.

The Role of AI in Idea Generation

In the ever-evolving landscape of innovation, artificial intelligence is proving to be a groundbreaking catalyst in generating ideas. It doesn't merely mimic human thought processes; it augments and redefines them, pushing boundaries that were once thought to be immutable. But how does a machine, devoid of emotional and sensory experience, contribute to the genesis of ideas typically considered a human forte? The answer lies not in replication but in augmentation, allowing creatives to leap beyond their traditional limitations.

AI is a unique partner in brainstorming, offering a digital collaborator that brings diverse perspectives and associations to the table. By processing vast amounts of data at lightning speed, AI can identify patterns and connections that might take humans significantly longer to discern, if at all. This ability transforms AI into a reservoir overflowing with potential ideas, ready to be explored and refined by human hands. It's akin to having an ever-present muse, one that's tireless and perpetually inventive.

Imagine a painter searching for a novel concept. The traditional approach might involve painstaking experimentation with colors, forms, and styles, often leading through long hours of trial and error. AI steps into this creative process not to dictate but to suggest; it can propose color palettes based on analyzed art trends or generate new abstract shapes inspired by historical art movements. The creative retains control, yet gains a panoramic view of possibilities that were previously obscured by human limits.

There's a certain serendipity in AI-driven idea generation. Its ability to produce unexpected combinations makes it an invaluable tool for those looking to break free from the constraints of conventional thinking. For instance, AI can mash together disparate concepts—like combining classical architecture with futuristic aesthetics—resulting in a hybrid form that ignites further creative exploration. This emergent creativity is something that was traditionally reliant on human intuition alone.

The utility of AI in idea generation also extends into more structured fields of creativity, such as marketing and design. In advertising, AI can analyze audience behavior and preferences to develop campaign ideas that resonate deeply with target demographics. By predicting trends and consumer tastes with remarkable accuracy, AI empowers creatives to craft messages that are both innovative and relevant.

There's something profoundly inspiring about witnessing AI transcend its status as a tool to become a co-creator. It prompts a re-evaluation of what it means to be creative and challenges long-held notions of originality and ownership. Rather than diminishing the role of the creative, AI complements their skills, offering insights that may not have been previously visible. This synergy underscores the notion that creativity knows no boundaries and can emerge from the confluence of human imagination and machine efficiency.

Moreover, AI is not just a tool for the solitary artist; it's reshaping collaborative dynamics within creative teams and industries. Imagine a room filled with designers, each bringing their unique perspective to the project. Now, introduce AI as a participant that can rapidly iterate design concepts or offer data-driven feedback. This creates a rich tapestry of ideas, collaboratively woven by both human and machine—a testament to the vitality of diversity in creativity.

However, the embrace of AI in idea generation isn't without its challenges. There's an ethical dimension to consider, especially regarding authorship and the authenticity of ideas generated by machines. Who owns an idea that's birthed with the assistance of AI, and how do we distinguish between machine-generated insights and human ones? These questions add layers of complexity to the discourse on creativity but also spurn innovation by demanding thoughtful exploration.

In embracing AI for idea generation, creatives are forging new paths where technology meets artistry. The fusion of logic and imagination expands the horizons of possibility, encouraging creatives to venture into the unknown with confidence. It's an era where innovation knows no bounds, where even the wildest of ideas can find a place in reality thanks to the collaborative spirit of AI.

This burgeoning partnership invites us to ponder the limits of artistic ingenuity and the expansive role AI can play in redefining these limits. With machines by our side, we are witnessing the dawn of a new epoch in creativity—one brimming with infinite possibilities, yet intimately shaped by both human vision and computational prowess.

Chapter 13:
The Impact on Traditional Artists

As AI continues to permeate the creative landscape, traditional artists find themselves at a crossroads. Many grapple with the rapid shift, torn between skepticism and curiosity about AI's potential to complement or overshadow their work. There's an undeniable tension as age-old techniques confront digital innovation, forcing artists to reconsider their place in this evolving ecosystem. Some adopt these tools, merging AI with traditional artistry to craft hybrid expressions; others remain steadfast, championing the authenticity of human-crafted art. The dialogue within the artistic community is charged with both trepidation and excitement, as creators weigh the transformative possibilities against the intrinsic value of human touch. Adaptability becomes a key theme, as artists who embrace change often see AI not as a replacement but as an extension of their creative potential, opening doors to previously unimagined artistic frontiers.

Reactions from the Artistic Community

The advent of artificial intelligence in the creative domain has sparked a myriad of reactions from the artistic community, ranging from intrigue and enthusiasm to apprehension and resistance. This diverse tapestry of response reflects the profound impact AI is having on traditional artists, challenging long-held beliefs about creativity, originality, and the very definition of art. As AI technology continues to evolve, so too do the perspectives and conversations within the artistic community.

Many artists first encountered AI with skepticism. The notion that machines, lacking human emotion and experience, could produce genuine art appeared unfathomable. These artists questioned how a series of algorithms could ever replicate the depth of human creativity or the nuanced process that human artists undergo. For them, art has always been deeply personal, a reflection of an individual's unique journey and emotions. Yet, AI seemed to challenge this conception, proposing that creativity might also emerge from data-driven processes.

Despite initial skepticism, curiosity among some artists began to grow. A portion of the community saw AI not as a threat but as a potential collaborator. They explored how AI could augment traditional artistic techniques, offering new tools for expression. This interest in collaboration wasn't about replacing the artist but about enhancing their capabilities, pushing creative boundaries beyond what had been previously imagined. For these artists, AI became a partner in an ongoing dialogue between human intuition and computational power.

On the other hand, there's a profound sense of anxiety among traditional artists. The ability of AI to produce artworks that mimic or even exceed human capabilities in certain styles and forms triggers fears of redundancy. Artists who have spent years honing their craft worry about being overshadowed by machines capable of producing works with less effort and in significantly less time. This fear isn't unfounded in a world that's constantly looking to optimize and economize.

Compounding this anxiety is the issue of originality. The training datasets that AI models rely upon often include works by human artists. Some artists express frustration and ethical concerns about AI generating art by leveraging existing human creations without proper acknowledgment or compensation. The question of ownership of AI-generated art remains a hotly debated topic. For many, this challenges the very notion of what it means to be an artist in an age where machines can replicate human styles so faithfully.

Amidst these concerns, certain artists champion the democratizing potential of AI. These proponents argue that, by lowering the barriers to entry, AI tools empower more people to create art, regardless of their traditional skills. The expanded accessibility could foster more diversity in the art world, as individuals from all walks of life have the means to express themselves creatively. This inclusivity brings a hopeful vision to AI's role, aligning with broader artistic values of exploration and inclusivity.

Indeed, some artists have reported feeling liberated by AI's capabilities. By automating aspects of the creative process, artists can focus on the conception and evolution of ideas rather than get bogged down by repetitive tasks. This notion of liberation reflects an optimistic view that embraces technological collaboration as a gateway to a new kind of creative freedom, where the mundane is lifted from the shoulders of artists, allowing for greater experimentation and innovation.

The artistic community also contemplates the cultural implications of integrating AI into art. There's a growing discourse on how AI might influence artistic identities and global art movements. Some fear the homogenization of art styles as algorithms replicate popular aesthetics, potentially stifling individuality. Conversely, other artists envision a new renaissance—an era of novel genres and hybrid forms born out of the marriage between human creativity and machine learning.

Then there are those who focus on the experiential aspect of AI art. These artists are interested in how AI can engage audiences in interactive and ever-evolving ways, pushing the envelope of what art exhibitions can look like. They see potential in creating artworks that adapt in real time, responding to viewers' emotions or interactions, thus transforming passive audiences into active participants.

The evolution of AI art prompts a reconsideration of how art is valued. Machine-generated works pose questions about the intrinsic value of art not solely dependent on human effort. Some artists challenge traditional market valuations and question whether art should be viewed primarily through the lens of labor or output. The ongoing evaluation of value in art is yet another facet of the community's reaction to AI.

In many ways, the artistic community's response to AI is a microcosm of a broader societal conversation about technology's place in our lives. The artist, long perceived as a lone genius, now navigates a landscape where collaboration with non-humans is possible, perhaps even necessary. This paradigm shift requires openness to reimagining traditional relationships between humans and their creations.

Ultimately, the artistic community remains divided, mirroring the multifaceted nature of AI's impact. Yet, it is in these divisions and discussions that the potential for growth lies. As artists continue to explore, adapt, and redefine their roles in an AI-augmented world, they may find themselves at the forefront of an artistic evolution, blending the timeless essence of humanity with the transformative power of technology.

Adaptation and Acceptance

As AI continues to revolutionize creative fields, the impact on traditional artists is both profound and multifaceted. Caught in the flux of this technological advance, some artists stand at a crossroads, deliberating whether to embrace these tools or to retreat to the comfort of classic methodologies. While the shift towards AI might initially seem daunting, adaptation and acceptance are emerging as pathways to not only survive but thrive in this redefined landscape.

The willingness to adapt often starts with a subtle mindset shift. Artists who are open to exploring AI tend to view it as an extension of their creative toolkit rather than a threatening replacement of their craft. By recognizing AI's potential to augment rather than supplant human creativity, artists can begin to reframe this technological invasion as an invitation to innovate, explore, and perhaps reach new levels of artistry that were previously unimaginable. In this way, adaptation becomes less about relinquishing traditional skills and more about integrating new ones.

Acceptance, however, doesn't translate to unconditional embrace. It involves a discerning approach where artists actively evaluate which aspects of AI resonate with their creative vision and practice. For sculptors, it might mean using AI to simulate models before chiseling away at marble, while illustrators might employ AI-driven color palette suggestions to enhance their original designs. Through selective adaptation, artists retain their authentic voices while allowing technology to enhance their expression.

Residencies and workshops dedicated to AI in art have started cropping up, providing traditional artists with the resources and community to explore these technologies. These environments often foster experimentation, allowing artists to engage with AI on their own terms in a supportive setting. Importantly, such initiatives create a culture of dialogue rather than division, where knowledge and experience are shared without the pressure to immediately produce AI-enhanced work.

Economic incentives also play a significant role in driving adaptation. As the market for AI-driven art grows, opportunities arise for artists to monetize their work in new ways. Digital art on blockchain platforms, AI-assisted commissions, and even collaborations with AI developers open doors to revenue streams beyond traditional gallery sales. On a practical level, this economic reality can motivate artists to engage with AI, not just out of creative curiosity, but also out of financial necessity.

The narrative surrounding AI and traditional artistry is not just about individual adaptation but also about collective acceptance within the artistic community. Artists' unions and creative collectives are beginning to discuss ethical standards, fair representation, and the cultural implications of AI in art. This collective dialogue is crucial in sculpting a balanced future where traditional art practices and AI-enhanced creations can coexist harmoniously.

Still, the path to acceptance is not without friction. Concerns about losing the human touch in art, the fear that AI will dilute authenticity and emotional depth, are valid and require ongoing discussion. Many artists lean into this discomfort, using it as a catalyst for creativity. They allow these concerns to inspire new works that comment on the interface of technology and humanity, using their art as a space for dialogue and reflection.

This embrace of AI by traditional artists is not uniform; it is marked by varying degrees of eagerness and resistance. There are pioneers who enthusiastically integrate deep learning algorithms into their process, while others carefully navigate their interaction with AI, mindful of maintaining their unique artistic identity. It's this diversity of adaptation methods that enriches the artistic ecosystem, allowing for a wide array of practices that can appeal to different tastes and audiences.

Educational institutions are also beginning to play a crucial role in this adaptation phase. By incorporating AI literacy into curricula, they equip the next generation of artists with both the technical skills and critical perspective needed to navigate a tech-driven creative environment. These programs are vital in normalizing AI as a creative partner, ensuring that future artists view it as a natural component of their artistic development.

Ultimately, the adaptation and acceptance of AI in the realm of traditional art rest upon a balance: the familiar roots of artistry merging with the digital branches of the future. By shifting paradigms and fostering a growth mindset, artists are beginning to see AI as a collaborative ally, one that can enhance human creativity in unprecedented ways. This integration promises not only a bright future for traditional art but an evolution that celebrates the unique capabilities of human and machine creativity alike.

Chapter 14:
AI and Creative Education

As the creative landscape undergoes a seismic transformation, AI is carving out a pivotal role in the education of tomorrow's artists and designers. It's reshaping curricula, urging educational institutions to integrate cutting-edge technologies that align with an AI-driven world. This shift demands not just new tools, but also a fresh approach to cultivating creative skills, blending traditional art forms with digital innovations. Students are no longer merely passive recipients of knowledge; they're becoming dynamic explorers in a world where art and technology converge. By encouraging experimentation and collaboration between human creativity and machine intelligence, educational programs are empowering a new generation to push boundaries and redefine the standards of artistic expression. This fusion of AI and creative education promises to unleash untamed potential, ensuring that the creators of tomorrow are not only adept with brushes and code but equipped with the foresight and adaptability to navigate an ever-evolving creative ecosystem.

Impacts on Art and Design Curricula

As artificial intelligence rapidly infiltrates various facets of our creative world, art and design education stands at the cusp of significant evolution. The incorporation of AI into curricula is not just a trend but a profound shift that challenges educational institutions to rethink and retool traditional teaching methodologies. This change offers a wealth of opportunities for students to engage with emerging technologies and equips them with skills that will be crucial in an increasingly AI-driven creative industry.

Art and design curricula around the globe are undergoing a transformation to include AI as a core component. Traditional art schools are recognizing that to prepare students for the future, they must embed technology and interdisciplinary learning into their programs. No longer can art education be solely about mastering paints and canvases or designing buildings with pencil and paper. Instead, it must embrace digital tools and AI technologies that redefine creative processes and outputs.

Integrating AI into art and design education fosters a new form of creative literacy. Students are encouraged to understand and employ AI as a tool that can augment human creativity rather than replace it. This involves educating students on the principles behind AI technologies, such as machine learning algorithms and neural networks, which directly impact artistic creation and design innovation.

Moreover, this educational shift towards AI helps cultivate an adaptive mindset among students. As they encounter AI-driven tools and platforms, they learn to be flexible and innovative, characteristics essential for thriving in modern creative industries. By working alongside AI, students gain proficiency in using technology to enhance aesthetic expression and design efficiency. For instance, with machine learning, design students can explore endless iterations of a concept, testing variations that may not have been feasible manually.

Another noteworthy impact of AI on art and design curricula is the emphasis on collaboration between disciplines. Previously, art and design students might focus solely on their specific areas of study. However, with AI in the mix, there's an increased convergence of fields such as technology, data science, and visual arts. This interdisciplinary approach encourages students to work beyond traditional boundaries, promoting a deeper understanding of AI's role in solving complex creative challenges.

The evolution of curricula also brings ethical considerations into the conversation. As students interact with AI, it's vital they understand the ethical implications of AI-generated creations. This includes discussions around authenticity, authorship, and the socio-political impacts of AI in art and design. By introducing these topics, educators are not only preparing students technically but also socially and ethically for the consequences of their work in broader society.

While AI presents new opportunities, it also poses challenges to educators, who must think critically about how to integrate technology without diminishing traditional artistic skills. Balancing these two elements is crucial. The goal is not to overshadow classical arts with technological advances but to complement and enhance them. Educators need to navigate how much emphasis to place on these new technologies, ensuring students are well-rounded in both classical techniques and modern AI-enabled practices.

Furthermore, the inclusion of AI in curricula nurtures a spirit of experimentation. Students are empowered to challenge existing paradigms by using AI to explore unconventional art forms and design concepts. They can push creative boundaries, imagining new possibilities that live at the intersection of human intuition and artificial capability. This spirit of innovation is key as it helps students carve out unique niches in a competitive creative landscape.

Ultimately, the integration of AI in art and design education represents more than just academic evolution. It signifies a broader cultural shift that acknowledges the symbiotic relationship between humanity and technology in the arts. By embracing this change, educational institutions are ensuring that the next generation of artists and designers are not only prepared to survive in an AI-enhanced world but are poised to lead and shape it.

As art and design schools continue to pioneer this integration, they lay the groundwork for a future where AI is seen less as a futuristic anomaly and more as an essential component of creative practice. It's a future where AI will not only coexist with human creativity but actively enable new forms of artistic expression and innovation. This movement doesn't just revolutionize curricula; it changes the landscape of what we can achieve at the intersection of art, design, and technology.

Developing New Creative Skills for the AI Era

As artificial intelligence continues to permeate the creative industries, it's crucial for creative professionals to adapt by developing new skills that align with this technological evolution. The landscape is changing rapidly, with AI no longer just encroaching on technical tasks but also venturing boldly into traditionally human domains such as art, design, and storytelling. It's not enough to just acknowledge AI's capabilities; creatives need to embrace and integrate these tools to unlock new realms of imagination and innovation.

The first vital skill in this AI era is understanding how to interact with AI systems themselves. While some creatives may shy away from the technical aspects, a foundational comprehension of how AI algorithms operate can be immensely beneficial. This doesn't necessarily mean becoming a coder overnight, but rather learning how these systems collect data, recognize patterns, and produce outputs. For example, knowing the fundamentals of machine learning can enhance a designer's ability to use AI tools effectively, ensuring that the outputs are both innovative and aligned with their vision.

Moreover, creativity in the AI era demands collaboration skills—in particular, the ability to work alongside machines as partners rather than mere tools. This requires a shift in mindset: viewing AI as a co-creator that can spark new ideas, test out multiple options in seconds, and even challenge human assumptions. Many design studios and filmmakers have already begun incorporating AI assistants to streamline workflows, experiment with fresh styles, and explore narrative structures that were previously unimaginable.

Critical thinking and ethical reasoning are also paramount. AI can present creatives with endless possibilities, but not all generated ideas will be suitable or ethical. Artists and designers must develop the ability to discern the cultural, social, and moral implications of their AI-assisted creations. This involves questioning biases inherent in the data sets AI systems are trained on and contemplating how these biases might manifest in the output. As AI becomes more deeply integrated into the creative process, the need for ethical scrutiny intensifies, reinforcing the human role as the moral compass in these collaborations.

AI's capacity for continuous learning and adaptation means it can provide creatives with real-time feedback. This offers an unprecedented opportunity for skill improvement, but it requires creatives to be open to iterative processes and ready to pivot based on new insights. Rather than seeing feedback as criticism, creatives must cultivate resilience and a growth mindset, seeing these adjustments as pathways to enhance their artistic practice.

Additionally, the integration of AI into creative professions necessitates a multidisciplinary approach. Artists and designers might find themselves collaborating with data scientists, engineers, and technologists. By engaging with diverse fields, creatives can widen their own skill sets, incorporating new perspectives and knowledge into their work. This cross-pollination can lead to genuinely innovative outcomes that push the boundaries of art and design.

The rise of AI also implies an increased demand for storytelling skills, albeit of a new variety. AI-generated content can struggle to resonate emotionally, which is where human ingenuity shines. Creatives must hone the ability to infuse stories with authenticity and emotional depth, ensuring that narratives crafted with AI touch audiences in profound ways. This isn't just about crafting compelling stories but also about leveraging AI to enhance storytelling by uncovering new angles and perspectives.

Moreover, creatives need to develop the dexterity to navigate an array of AI tools, each with its own strengths and limitations. Familiarity with a range of software and platforms can be a considerable advantage, enabling artists to choose the best tools for different aspects of their projects. This might include AI systems designed for image recognition, natural language processing, or generative design, each offering unique functionalities to augment creative workflows.

There's a growing necessity for resilience in the face of rapid technological change. The question is less about *if* AI will transform the creative industries and more about *how* it will. To stay relevant, creatives must be ready to adopt new technologies swiftly and effectively, adapting their skills and approaches as AI continues to evolve. This dynamic process is about staying curious and being willing to experiment with what AI can do, rather than clinging to the status quo.

The skills necessary for creative professionals in the AI era are not just new but transformative, opening pathways for innovation that were unimaginable just a few decades ago. As AI continues to evolve, so must the skills of those who wield it creatively. By embracing AI's potential, creatives are poised not only to survive but to thrive in a reshaped artistic landscape, ready to contribute to a future where the definition of creativity itself is ever-expanding.

Finally, it's vital for educational systems to keep pace with these changes, developing curricula that prepare the next generation of creatives for a world where human and machine creativity coexist. This might mean encouraging students to engage directly with AI tools, fostering an understanding of both their capabilities and limitations, and nurturing the capacity to critique AI-generated content thoughtfully. Moreover, teaching young creatives the importance of maintaining their unique human touch in a digital age is crucial. After all, the most profound and impactful art will always be that which integrates the best of both worlds: the infinite possibilities of AI and the irreplaceable depth of human emotion and experience.

Chapter 15:
AI in Visual Arts

In recent years, AI has made a profound impact on visual arts, transforming traditional boundaries and enabling artists to explore uncharted territories of creativity. Machine learning algorithms and neural networks are now pivotal tools that artists use to manipulate images and generate novel visual experiences. These technologies allow for remarkable experimentation with form, color, and composition, offering a new palette for artistic expression. While AI can autonomously create, it often shines brightest when it becomes a collaborator with human artists, enhancing their ability to transcend the limits of conventional practice. As creatives let algorithms explore realms beyond human intuition, the result is a vibrant interplay of imagination, where the machine becomes an ally in the artistic process. This evolving landscape challenges us to reconsider notions of originality and authorship, inviting a reimagined dialogue between tradition and innovation in the visual arts.

Machine Learning and Image Manipulation

In the expanding landscape of artificial intelligence within the visual arts, machine learning and image manipulation stand out as transformative forces. These technologies are reshaping not only the tools and processes artists use but also challenging the very nature of creative expression. By analyzing patterns and generating new ideas, machine learning algorithms offer innovative possibilities previously unimaginable.

At the heart of image manipulation lies the neural network—a network reminiscent of the human brain's structure and function, equipped to learn from swathes of visual data. These networks are the engine behind many modern advancements. Convolutional neural networks (CNNs), for example, excel at image recognition and rendering tasks, deciphering intricate image details and transforming them creatively. Artists and designers can leverage these capabilities to explore unique aesthetics, pushing boundaries beyond traditional methods.

The ability of AI to generate and manipulate images isn't just about enhancing existing processes; it's a catalyst for creating entirely new art forms. From style transfer—where an AI can apply the texture and color patterns of a renowned painting to a photograph—to more complex applications like generating hyper-realistic images of imaginary landscapes, the potential is vast. These technologies provide artists with a powerful toolkit to express concepts and emotions that might have remained locked in their minds without such technological interventions.

However, the ease of manipulating images in ways that blur reality raises critical questions. The ethical dimension of image manipulation through AI is multifaceted, encompassing issues such as the authenticity of AI-generated images and the potential for misuse in creating misleading visuals. When it comes to art, an area already rich in subjective interpretations, these questions become even more complex. It calls for a dialogue on how we define originality and authorship in an age where machines are active participants in the creative process.

Despite these complexities, AI-based image manipulation has democratized access to powerful creative tools. Previously reserved for those with extensive skills in digital art, such techniques are now available to amateur creatives, thanks to user-friendly applications that simplify complex processes. This democratization empowers more diverse voices to contribute to the cultural tapestry, making visual arts more inclusive than ever before.

Moreover, the collaboration between human intuition and machine precision illuminates new paths for artistic expression. The algorithms excel at generating novel patterns or recombining existing data in unexpected ways, creating an avenue for exploration and discovery. Artists can guide these processes, infusing their unique sensibilities and intentions into the final output. It's a dialogue between artist and algorithm—a new way to converse with technology, where the unpredictable becomes a source of inspiration.

Looking forward, advancements in machine learning promise to enhance image manipulation even further, with AI capable of understanding and even predicting aesthetic preferences. Such developments might allow AI not only to follow instructions but also to co-create with artists based on inferred preferences and styles. As the technology matures, it will continue to refine our understanding of 'art,' challenging our historical notions and stretching the limits of creativity.

In education, the impact is transformative as well. As these technologies become more ingrained, art and design curricula worldwide are evolving to incorporate AI tools, offering students the chance to experiment with machine learning as a medium. By fostering an environment where traditional skills coexist with cutting-edge technology, educational institutions are preparing the next generation of creatives to innovate and inspire.

The journey of machine learning and image manipulation in the visual arts is just beginning. With each new algorithm and application, the vast potential of AI in art expands, inviting us to explore its implications deeply and thoughtfully. It's a call to rethink our engagement with imagery and the stories we tell through it, urging us to embrace the limitless possibilities at the intersection of human creativity and technological prowess.

Ultimately, machine learning's role in image manipulation is not just about what machines can do, but about what humanity can achieve when we combine our creativity with the power of AI. As artists and technologists continue to weave these technologies into the fabric of the creative industries, we stand on the cusp of an era where the impossible becomes possible, reshaping the artistic endeavors of today and tomorrow.

Creating Art with Neural Networks

Art has always been a realm of boundless creativity and expression. With the advent of artificial intelligence, particularly neural networks, this landscape has dramatically evolved, paving new paths for innovation and exploration in visual arts. Neural networks, a backbone of AI technology, simulate the way human brains perceive, understand, and generate complex patterns. They're not just algorithms; they're a revolutionary tool capable of crafting art that elicits human-like responses, pushing the boundaries of imagination further than ever before.

At its core, a neural network is an interconnected assembly of nodes, or "neurons," that mimic biological neural systems. These systems are embedded with layers capable of processing vast amounts of data, understanding patterns, and generating original outputs. Picture a painter with an infinite palette; that's what a neural network can be when it's tasked with creating art. By training on extensive datasets of images, a network can learn and synthesize unique art forms, echoing styles from classic to contemporary and beyond.

The power of neural networks in generating art can be seen in projects like DeepArt, among others. These endeavors have demonstrated neural networks' potential to reinterpret famous paintings through distinctive lenses, merging the boundaries between what is considered traditional art and what is possible with AI. These networks can analyze a photograph, absorb the stylistic nuances of a piece by Van Gogh or Monet, and reimagine an entirely new creation that feels both familiar and foreign.

A breakthrough moment in AI art was the appearance of Generative Adversarial Networks (GANs), a specialized form of neural networks that have played a significant role in evolving how AI creates. GANs consist of two networks - a generator and a discriminator - doing a remarkable job at creating authentic-looking images. While the generator strives to craft art, the discriminator acts as a curator, assessing the authenticity of the art against real-world standards. This push-pull dynamic is akin to an artist refining their work until it reaches aesthetic perfection.

One of the most captivating aspects of neural networks is their ability to transcend the typical constraints faced by human artists, such as physical limits or rigid historical narratives. Neural networks don't just mimic; they adapt and evolve. They can explore abstract realms and produce mind-bending visual experiences that challenge viewers' perceptions, inviting them to question reality and representation in novel ways.

This new modality has redefined the notion of creativity. It allows collaborative workflows where artists, designers, and technologists come together to push creative limits. AI-generated art raises an intriguing question: where does the artist end and the machine begin? This question doesn't diminish the value of creations formed with AI support; if anything, it enriches the discourse around the very nature of art and creativity in a technological age.

Moreover, neural networks are not just isolated tools but part of a larger ecosystem that embraces other AI models and creative fields. They interlace with AI-driven animation, motion graphics, and even augmented reality, providing a multifaceted canvas for new-age artists. This convergence is opening doors to interactive art forms where the audience, not just the creator, becomes a part of the unfolding artistic narrative.

Critics might argue that AI can't genuinely "create," as it lacks consciousness or emotional insight. However, the absence of these human attributes doesn't detract from the significance of AI-generated art. Instead, it highlights a fundamental shift in understanding art's purpose and the diverse agencies behind its creation. Neural networks allow us to question our definitions of originality and authorship, fostering a more inclusive dialogue surrounding artistic merit and innovation.

While neural networks are tools brimming with potential, the technology is not without its challenges. Issues related to ethical considerations, ownership disputes, and authenticity continue to surface as AI art gains prevalence. Where does the credit lie—should it be given to the algorithm, the programmer, or the artistic direction provided by humans? These are pertinent discussions that shape our understanding of AI's role in art and society.

Yet, it's essential to look at these challenges not as barriers but as opportunities to forge new paths for creativity and art curation. By acknowledging and addressing these concerns, we can sculpt an artistic landscape where AI and human creativity coexist harmoniously, each amplifying the other's strengths. This collaboration can spawn unique styles and expressions, sparking inspiration and curiosity even among skeptics.

As we continue to spearhead development in AI-driven art, neural networks will undoubtedly remain pivotal in guiding these explorations. This isn't merely a technological advancement; it is a cultural change that remolds our perception of artistic pursuit. As with every evolution, the integration of neural networks in art requires adapting without forsaking the emotional and conceptual depths that define our artistic heritage.

The journey of creating art with neural networks is only beginning, and the results are already spectacular. Art will always be an intimate reflection of human experience, but AI's evolving capability invites us to expand this narrative, share the canvas, and embrace a future where art knows no bounds. By intertwining algorithmic prowess with human ingenuity, the horizon of creative possibilities broadens, inviting us all to dream bigger and create fearlessly.

Chapter 16:
Music Composition with AI

As we journey into the realm of music composition with artificial intelligence, we uncover a landscape where technology and creativity entwine, redefining what it means to create music. AI's influence in the music industry is not merely about producing melodies or rhythms; it's about fostering a new form of collaboration between human artists and intelligent algorithms. Musicians are increasingly working alongside AI to push the boundaries of sonic exploration, crafting sounds that challenge conventional notions and trigger a profound emotional response. This chapter explores how AI tools harness vast databases of musical knowledge and intricate learning algorithms to offer composers a palette of unprecedented possibilities, from generating entire compositions to suggesting unique harmonies and melodies. The synergy between human intuition and AI's computational prowess opens doors to innovation, inspiring creatives to venture beyond familiar territories. This evolution is not just transformative but also democratizing, allowing artists from diverse backgrounds to experiment and express themselves in novel ways. In doing so, AI is not replacing human musicians; rather, it's expanding their canvas, inviting a new era of musical creativity that resonates with the limitless potential and diversity of human imagination.

Transforming Sounds: AI's Musical Influence

AI's incursion into the realm of music composition marks an evolutionary leap in how we perceive, create, and interact with sound. The art of music has always been a reflection of the human condition, a tapestry of emotions woven through notes and rhythms. AI challenges this notion, offering a new language for sound by reimagining how music can be crafted and experienced.

Machine learning algorithms have empowered AI with the ability to analyze vast datasets of musical works from different genres, eras, and cultures. This capability enables AI to uncover patterns that might elude the human composer, offering novel combinations and stylistic fusions. Not only does this yield fresh compositions, but it also allows a re-interpretation of traditional music, breathing new life into classic tunes while maintaining their foundational essence.

Consider the role of AI as a collaborator rather than a mere tool. AI doesn't just replicate existing musical forms; it actively engages in the creation process, suggesting harmonies, rhythms, and structures that might otherwise remain unexplored. This symbiotic relationship between human and machine pushes creative boundaries, opening up pathways previously deemed unimaginable. Musicians can now explore complex symphonic arrangements without traditional training, guided instead by AI's suggestions.

The capacity of AI to generate music transcending human emotion is both a point of fascination and contention. AI can mimic the emotive qualities of music by recognizing and replicating the elements that typically evoke specific feelings in listeners. For some, this represents AI's potential to touch the heart of human experience. Yet, others argue whether these emotions generated by AI are genuine or merely a digital facsimile.

Amidst these developments, the question of authorship arises. Who owns the creations born from AI's virtual hands? The algorithms themselves? The engineers who designed them? Or the musicians who fed them data? These debates redefine notions of ownership in creative works, inviting industry leaders to rethink traditional legal frameworks in the music industry.

AI's impact extends beyond creation to transformation. With technology, we can remaster old recordings with unprecedented clarity, alter vocal styles, and produce remixes that transcend the original artist's vision. This flexibility allows seasoned artists to reintroduce their work to new audiences, ensuring their legacy resonates across generations.

AI also democratizes musical creation. By lowering entry barriers, anyone with a computer can become a music producer. This democratization fosters inclusivity, allowing voices from diverse backgrounds to partake in the creative process, and paving the way for cultural fusions that spotlight global diversity.

The ethical considerations surrounding AI-generated music warrant attention. The balance between originality and assistance is delicate. AI can inadvertently propagate biases present in the datasets it learns from, skewing the authenticity of its output. Vigilance in dataset selection and algorithm tuning becomes essential to preserve ethical integrity.

In performance, AI complements human artists, offering live improvisation possibilities that were once limited by human unpredictability. The fusion of AI with live improvisation allows for performances that are dynamically reactive, adjusting to audience responses in real time, thus heightening the interactive concert experience.

While AI's presence in music is undeniably transformative, it is not without limitations. Critics emphasize the lack of soul or the ineffable quality of music produced artificially, prompting discussion on what constitutes genuine artistry. AI lacks the life experiences that inform the deeply personal expressions often found in human-made music.

Looking towards the future, the continued evolution of AI in music composition beckons us to consider the implications for musical education and careers. Will the role of the musician shift from creator to curator, guiding AI to achieve desired outcomes? The roles and skills associated with music are set to evolve, calling for adaptive educational approaches.

Ultimately, AI's role in transforming sounds and music composition is a testament to the vast potential of human-machine collaboration. It is an exploration of technology's ability to act as an extension of our creative faculties, challenging us to rethink and redefine what music is and what it could be. As technology progresses, the symphonic dance between AI and artistry continues to unfold, inspiring curiosity, debate, and innovation.

Collaborations Between AI and Musicians

The intersection of artificial intelligence and music composition is a burgeoning field where traditional methods are being stretched and reimagined. Musicians and AI systems are beginning to coalesce in creative partnerships, challenging our notions of what it means to compose music. This synergy is not just about AI taking over compositional tasks but about creating a new landscape where musicians and machines collaborate to produce works that push the boundaries of creativity. From generating new sounds to assisting in composition, the partnership between musicians and AI is multifaceted and evolving.

One of the most significant arenas of collaboration lies in the use of AI tools to assist musicians in the compositional process. These tools can analyze vast amounts of music, identifying patterns and offering suggestions that can lead to new creative directions. For instance, AI can generate melodies or harmonies based on a specific style or genre and present these as options for musicians to explore. This doesn't diminish the role of the musician; rather, it enhances their creative process, providing new unique ideas that they may not have conceived independently.

Moreover, AI's ability to handle complex data sets allows it to simulate distinct instruments or even entire orchestras, offering musicians and composers a digital playground to experiment with sounds and arrangements. This capability is particularly beneficial for composers who might not have immediate access to live orchestras or professional studios. By enabling detailed simulations, AI democratizes music production, making high-quality composition accessible to a broader audience.

Beyond mere assistance in composing, AI is taking on more engaging roles in live performances. Certain musicians are experimenting with AI systems that interact in real-time during concerts, creating dynamic compositions that evolve with the audience's energy and reactions. In these performances, AI doesn't just follow a pre-set algorithm but responds to live input, adding an improvisational element to the music. This kind of collaboration transforms concerts into uniquely ephemeral experiences where each performance is distinct, shaped by the collaborative interplay between human and machine.

An intriguing aspect of these collaborations is how AI is used for remixing and reinterpreting existing musical works. With AI's ability to dissect and analyze music on a micro-level, it can recombine elements of a track in innovative ways, offering fresh perspectives on traditional compositions. Musicians are thus empowered to reinterpret their work or the works of others, exploring variations that might have remained unexplored in a purely human-driven process. This capability highlights AI's role as both collaborator and co-creator, blending predefined rules with exploratory techniques.

It's not just in production and performance where AI is making an impact; it also plays a role in music education. Aspiring musicians can now compose and experiment with AI tools that teach through doing—offering feedback and instant demonstrations of complex musical theories. This hands-on approach can accelerate learning and inspire students by showing them the far-reaching possibilities of music creation beyond traditional boundaries.

Despite these advances, the collaboration between AI and musicians continues to be underpinned by ethical and philosophical discussions. Questions naturally arise regarding attribution and artistic ownership, especially when AI contributes significantly to a piece's creation. Who owns a composition when it's the product of both human intuition and machine learning algorithms? Musicians and technologists are wrestling with these questions, exploring copyright models and ethical frameworks that can accommodate AI's growing role in the creative process.

The aesthetic outcomes of these collaborations also beg reflection. AI introduces styles and methods that often challenge traditional musical aesthetics, offering listeners experiences that may initially feel foreign but gradually find a place within the broader musical landscape. As artists and listeners grow more familiar with AI's capabilities, the integration of artificial processes in music-making is increasingly appreciated not as a replacement for human creativity but as a new layer in the artistic hierarchy.

Ultimately, collaborations between AI and musicians testify to the vast potential of technology-enhanced creativity. As AI continues to evolve, its integration into musical processes will likely deepen, leading to further innovation in how music is conceived, produced, and performed. This trajectory offers a vivid example of how AI can act as a transformative force in creative fields, one that shares creative agency with human artists while challenging and expanding traditional understandings of what it means to create music.

In looking ahead, it will be essential for musicians, technologists, and audiences to remain engaged in dialogue, ensuring that collaborations between AI and musicians continue to respect and advance artistic integrity and cultural heritage. As this partnership develops, so too will the ways in which we understand and appreciate the art of music, opening doors to a future where the composition is a truly multidimensional collaboration.

Chapter 17:
The Business of AI Creativity

The intersection of AI and creativity has not only sparked a new artistic revolution but also transformed the business landscape of art and design. Embracing AI-powered creativity, industry leaders are reimagining the ways creations are monetized, distributing art that evolves beyond traditional confines. Visionaries in the field are forming strategic collaborations to navigate this brave new world, where the confluence of artifice and innovation amplifies creative potential. Amidst this transformation, an ecosystem of platforms is emerging, dedicated to the licensing, exhibition, and commercialization of AI-generated works, profoundly altering the market dynamics. As new players capitalize on AI's expansive capabilities, questions about ownership, valuation, and authenticity surface, urging businesses to establish frameworks that honor both ethics and creativity. As entrepreneurs and technologists look to the horizon, the pursuit of sustainable economic models for AI-driven art continues to inspire dynamic approaches that promise to reshape the creative industries for years to come.

Monetizing AI Art and Design

As AI stakes its claim in the realm of creativity, the monetization of AI-generated art and design emerges as a visionary yet intricate frontier. For creative professionals and industry leaders, this signifies not just an evolution in artistic techniques but a restructuring of traditional economic models. AI-generated art offers vast opportunities to capitalize on innovation, challenging the essence of originality while redefining value creation. It's no longer a question of *if* AI will impact the art and design market—it's about *how* and *to what extent*.

The initial steps toward monetizing AI art involve understanding the market dynamics and the unique value propositions these creations offer. In many ways, AI art disrupts the stereotype of creativity being a solely human endeavor. Artists now wield AI as a collaborative tool, amplifying their creative capabilities and enabling the production of artworks that transcend human imagination. This blend of man and machine takes the concept of art to new dimensions, where the works' novelty itself holds significant commercial appeal.

Another avenue ripe for exploration is the licensing of AI-generated designs. Designers can automate and customize designs extensively, aligning closely with clients' needs while maintaining high-efficiency levels. In an industry that prizes efficiency and creativity, AI tools offer an unparalleled advantage by allowing designers to deliver tailored solutions at scale. Negotiating rights and licensing agreements for these autonomous creations requires new legal frameworks, yet visionary professionals are already navigating these waters.

The use of AI in art and design presents unique ethical and ownership challenges, critical to its commercialization. Who owns an artwork created by an algorithm, and how do creators ensure they receive due credit and compensation? The answers aren't straightforward, and we find ourselves navigating a digital Wild West where legal precedents are yet to be established. Perhaps it's in this uncertainty where innovation thrives most, calling upon creative thinkers to reshape intellectual property norms and formulate strategies that balance profit with fairness.

The AI Muse

Moreover, AI art's ability to democratize the creative process cannot be overlooked. By lowering entry barriers, AI allows more individuals to participate meaningfully in art creation, manipulating algorithms to reflect their artistic vision. This democratization also unlocks new revenue streams, from direct sales to royalties from digital platforms hosting AI art. Art marketplaces are beginning to embrace AI art more fully, recognizing the audience's growing interest in these novel expressions.

Exploring persistent income models, such as subscription services that provide access to AI tools and artworks, represents another promising monetization pathway. This strategy aligns with a broader shift toward the subscription economy, providing a stable income source for creators and continuous engagement from consumers. Platforms offering generative design services can capitalize on a model that emphasizes access over ownership, appealing to a diverse clientele ranging from amateur creatives to established enterprises.

AI's role in branding and marketing further extends its commercial footprint. AI-generated designs personalized to consumer preferences create fresh opportunities to monetize creativity in advertising. By harnessing AI's analytical capabilities, brands craft highly personalized and dynamic marketing campaigns resonating deeply with target audiences, maximizing engagement and conversion rates.

Equally compelling is the secondary market potential for AI-generated works. As collectors begin recognizing the value of AI creativity, the market for retrading these assets expands, paralleling traditional art markets. The prospect of tokenizing digital art through blockchain technology ensures originality and provenance, potentially driving value appreciation over time. With collectors investing in AI artworks, the market anticipates unprecedented liquidity and growth.

Collaborations between AI artists and established creatives usher in another monetization stream through joint exhibitions and art projects. These partnerships allow traditional artists to diversify their portfolios while fostering inclusivity and innovation in the art world. Innovative exhibitions that combine AI installations with human artistry not only captivate audiences but translate into lucrative sponsorships and partnerships.

In the realm of education and training, monetizing AI art and design involves offering workshops and courses that teach the integration of AI into traditional creative processes. As demand for AI-centered skills grows, educational institutions and independent creators can capitalize on this shift by developing curriculum and training modules that impart critical knowledge, thereby generating substantial revenue while empowering the future workforce.

Thus, monetizing AI art and design is a multidimensional endeavor that calls for a balance of creativity, strategic foresight, and ethical consideration. As AI further assimilates into the creative industries, those who innovate will carve out robust markets, establishing new paradigms of aesthetic and economic value.

Industry Leaders and Innovators

In the rapidly evolving landscape of AI creativity, industry leaders and innovators are shaping the future of creative expression. These pioneering individuals and companies aren't just developing technology; they're redefining what it means to create. As AI becomes more ingrained in creative processes, these visionaries are exploring novel applications and pushing boundaries, sparking debates about the very essence of creativity and artistry.

Among the most influential figures in AI creativity, a few names stand out. OpenAI, for instance, has played a pivotal role in advancing how AI can generate text, images, and even music. Their work illustrates a commitment to exploring AI's potential to assist and inspire human creators. Through groundbreaking releases like GPT-3, they've shown that AI can produce text that's not only coherent but often insightful, blurring the lines between human and machine authorship.

Then there's DeepMind, Google's AI sister company, which is well-known for pushing the envelope in machine learning. Their foray into AI-assisted artistry includes neural networks capable of generating visuals from textual descriptions, providing artists with powerful new tools to visualize their ideas. This technology challenges traditional notions of image creation and encourages creatives to think beyond the canvas.

The fashion industry, too, is witnessing a transformative phase led by pioneers like the team behind IBM's Watson. Using AI to predict trends and personalize fashion experiences, they've revolutionized how designers approach collections. This melding of AI with haute couture exemplifies a partnership that's both pragmatic and visionary—streamlining production while expanding creative possibilities.

Startups also play a significant role in the AI art revolution. Companies like Runway ML and Artbreeder offer accessible platforms for creators of all skill levels to experiment with AI-driven art. By democratizing these tools, they empower a new generation of artists, emphasizing AI's role not as a replacement for creativity but as a catalyst for exploration and innovation.

It's crucial to highlight the human element in AI-driven creativity. Visionaries like Mario Klingemann, an artist who utilizes AI as both a medium and muse, draw attention to the symbiotic relationship between humans and machines. His work underscores the notion that AI isn't merely a tool for automation but an extension of artistic inquiry and expression, a viewpoint shared by many contemporary AI artists.

Furthermore, institutions like the San Francisco Museum of Modern Art and the Tate Modern in London have started incorporating AI-generated pieces into their collections, signaling a shift in how traditional art spaces engage with technological innovation. These institutions are fostering discussions about the value and authenticity of AI art, recognizing its growing importance in the cultural landscape.

In academia, universities like MIT and Stanford are at the forefront of researching AI's impact on creativity. By establishing interdisciplinary programs that merge art with AI, they prepare future generations to lead in an era where technology and creativity are intertwined. Their initiatives show the importance of fostering environments where creativity and computational prowess meet.

The efforts of these industry leaders and innovators are not without challenges. The ethical implications of machine-generated art, questions of authorship, and the digital divide in access to these technologies are just a few of the hurdles that the industry continues to grapple with. However, these challenges also present opportunities for setting new standards and creating inclusive spaces for all creators.

Amidst the technological marvels, it's essential to remember that creativity is deeply rooted in human experience. AI artistry, guided by these pioneering leaders, enriches rather than diminishes this experience. By embracing AI's potential and addressing its challenges, these innovators inspire a broader reconsideration of what art can be in the digital age.

Looking ahead, the path carved by these leaders will likely lead to even more interdisciplinary collaborations across technology, art, and media. This synergy will foster new creative methodologies and unexpected outcomes, challenging us to rethink the limitations of art and the definition of creativity itself. As AI continues to develop, so too will the roles of its industry leaders and innovators, standing at the helm of a creative renaissance.

Chapter 18:
Future Trends in AI Creativity

As we look to the horizon of AI creativity, we're witnessing the dawn of an era where the bounds of imagination start to blur into the capabilities of technology. The next wave of AI evolution in creative fields promises an integration that feels less like a tool and more akin to a symbiotic dance between man and machine. From real-time content generation tailored to individual tastes to AI artists that can intuitively collaborate with humans on ventures once deemed purely subjective, the landscape is poised for transformation. Cultural implications run deep, reshaping not just what we create, but also how we perceive creation itself, forging new paradigms in authenticity and originality. As AI's potential blooms, it challenges us to rethink art not as a static tradition but as a dynamic, evolving narrative that will redefine our collective artistic identity, urging creatives and technologists alike to venture boldly into uncharted territories. With each breakthrough, the path forward becomes both an ethical journey and an inspiring call to innovate, ensuring that AI's role in artistry is not only transformative but also profoundly human at its core.

Predicting the Next AI Evolutions

The realm of AI in creativity has already seen immense transformations, redefining how we conceive art, design, and media. As we look to the horizon, the evolution of AI promises even more radical changes - ones that might just revolutionize our entire creative landscape. The confluence of advancing technologies, expanding data repositories, and innovative algorithms paves the way for developments that were, not long ago, pure imagination. But what does the future really hold for AI in creativity, and how might these changes manifest?

First, we should consider the development of more sophisticated algorithms capable of producing creative outputs that not only imitate but also reinvent and transcend human ingenuity. These algorithms are increasingly becoming capable of understanding nuanced cultural and contextual cues, enabling them to create art that resonates on a deeply human level. Future iterations may draw from a vast array of cultural heritage databases, blending historical styles with futuristic interpretations, and offering fresh, hybrid art forms yet to be realized.

Moreover, the integration of AI with other cutting-edge technologies like virtual reality (VR) and augmented reality (AR) is likely to forge wholly immersive creative experiences. Imagine walking through a VR gallery where each painting transforms into a multidimensional, interactive narrative at the blink of an eye. AI, interfaced with AR, could allow for temporal art installations that morph in real-time based on viewer engagement and environmental factors. This potential for AI to create dynamic, evolving art experiences heralds a new era of audience interaction and participatory creation.

Beyond visual art, we can anticipate AI continuing to profoundly influence fields like music and literature. Composers and authors of the future might collaborate with AI to explore musical scales and narrative structures that were previously unimaginable. As AI systems gain more access to diverse musical traditions and literary canons around the world, they could synthesize these influences to craft innovative compositions and stories that appeal across cultural boundaries. AI-driven creativity could indeed become a unifying force, harmonizing global artistic expressions with unseen possibilities.

The evolution of AI in creativity doesn't stop at technical innovation. It will likely inspire shifts in the perception of artistic identity and authorship. As machines become co-creators, the lines between artist and tool will grow blurrier. This shift might necessitate new frameworks for understanding and categorizing creative output. Future art and media could challenge traditional definitions and ideas about what constitutes art or who deserves credit as the artist.

On a practical level, advancements in AI may lead to the democratization of creative tools. As AI capabilities become more accessible, artists across the globe, especially in underrepresented or resource-limited regions, could harness these technologies to create and share their visions. This democratization might ignite worldwide art movements and conversations that are yet to materialize, catalyzed by AI's unprecedented ability to equalize creative access.

AI's predictive power will also evolve, enabling deeper foresight into creative trends and audience preferences. By analyzing social media, streaming statistics, and cultural consumption patterns, AI could guide artists and creators towards future steps that align with evolving public tastes. This intelligence could influence everything from the colors in a painting to the chords in a symphony, making creativity more responsive and attuned to audience needs and wants.

However, with these exciting prospects come significant ethical considerations. The progression of AI in creativity must heed caution to balance innovation with ethical integrity. Questions about ownership, authenticity, and moral choices regarding the use of AI will mold future frameworks governing creative technologies. Ensuring AI acts as a tool for enhancement rather than replacement will be pivotal in maintaining a human-centric approach to artistic evolution.

Finally, AI's advancements will likely push the boundaries of creative education. As AI systems continue to break new ground in artistic exploration, educational institutions might need to reconsider the skills and knowledge needed for future creatives. Training programs may soon include AI literacy, equipping artists, designers, and media professionals with the wisdom to collaborate effectively with machines and craft AI-augmented artworks.

The next evolutions in AI creativity hold promise for unraveling uncharted artistic territories and augmenting human expression in unimaginable ways. As we stand on the brink of this next chapter, the convergence of creativity and artificial intelligence beckons us to embrace a future filled with collaboration, innovation, and endless possibility.

Long-Term Cultural Implications

In imagining the long-term cultural implications of AI in creativity, we find ourselves at a crossroads of potential and caution. Artificial intelligence, as it permeates the creative industries, is bound to shape not just the art and content we produce, but the very way we perceive creativity itself. In the framework of our cultural evolution, AI presents both a tool and a challenge, inviting us to reconsider notions of authorship, originality, and creativity. This dual aspect is likely to redefine what it means to be a creator, who becomes part of this narrative, and how cultural narratives themselves evolve.

The democratization of art facilitated by AI tools is one of the most profound cultural shifts already underway. As AI-powered platforms enable anyone to create sophisticated art, music, or stories, the barriers to entry are dramatically lowered. This inclusivity fosters a wider diversity of voices and ideas, enriching the cultural tapestry. Such accessibility could catalyze a new Renaissance, where the expression of ideas is not limited by traditional skill boundaries but is expanded through technology. However, this also poses the question of how we define artistic merit in a context where effort and expertise are complemented by AI capabilities. Will the value of art change in a landscape where technical skill is not a pre-requisite?

Moreover, the integration of AI in creativity is likely to lead to new artistic movements and genres, driven by the collaboration between humans and machines. Just as past technological advances like photography and digital art have birthed new forms, AI-powered creativity will undoubtedly inspire artistic innovations. These innovations may be characterized by a blending of human intuition with machine precision, resulting in works that neither species alone could conceive. The intersection of human emotions and AI's analytical prowess could lead to a hyper-realistic aesthetic or one that invites deeper introspection and philosophical inquiry.

The potential for AI to influence cultural narratives extends beyond the individual work of art—it encompasses collective understanding and the communication of shared experiences. Through the analysis of vast amounts of data, AI can identify and amplify emerging cultural trends, potentially even creating new paradigms of thought and expression. AI might well act as both an observer and a catalyst for cultural shifts, presenting narratives or themes that provoke societal reflection or change. In doing so, AI can help bridge cultural divides, offering new ways for global communities to connect and empathize through shared digital experiences.

Yet, as AI becomes more embedded in the fabric of creative industries, there are cultural risks to consider. Homogenization looms as a potential threat, where the prolific use of AI tools could lead to a cultural landscape dominated by algorithmically generated aesthetics and narratives. If not vigilantly curated and critically examined, the outputs of AI could lead to cultural clichés or stereotypes being perpetuated, overshadowing the nuanced diversity of human creativity. Thus, maintaining a balance between AI efficiency and the idiosyncratic nature of human expression will be critical in preserving cultural uniqueness.

The role of the creator is also poised for significant transformation. As AI assumes a position of partnership rather than mere tool, artists and creatives might need to redefine their identities and processes. This shift necessitates a cultural dialogue around authorship and ownership in art forms that are increasingly hybrid in nature. As creators navigate this new territory, the cultural emphasis may shift from the sole genius archetype to a more collective and interdisciplinary model of creativity, celebrating the synthesis between human and machine collaboration.

In education, AI's impact on creative curricula might have long-lasting cultural effects. Training future generations of artists to work alongside AI could foster a paradigm where technological literacy becomes an intrinsic aspect of the creative process. Consequently, cultural education may prioritize adaptability and the integration of AI tools, fostering a workforce that values collaboration over competition with machines.

The ethical considerations that arise from AI in creativity will also leave a cultural footprint. Questions about AI's autonomy, decision-making, and the ethical boundaries of its creativity will likely spur broad societal debate. This will challenge cultural norms related to accountability and empathy in art and design, as we strive to define the moral parameters of what AI should and shouldn't do in creative domains. Engaging with these discussions will be crucial to shaping equitable and human-centric cultural policies as AI's role in creation grows.

Looking forward, the long-term cultural implications of AI in creativity present both an exhilarating and daunting prospect. As AI technologies continue to evolve, their integration into creative processes offers the potential for unprecedented innovation and dynamic cultural evolution. However, the cultural ramifications of these changes call for careful consideration and stewardship, ensuring that the human element remains central in the narrative of AI advancements. By embracing the possibilities while mindfully managing the challenges, society can hope to harness AI's creative potential to enhance, rather than diminish, our rich cultural heritage.

Chapter 19:
Regional Perspectives and Diversity

As we voyage into the realm of AI creativity on a global scale, a rich tapestry of regional perspectives and diversity unfolds, highlighting how cultural nuances shape and are shaped by technological innovation. AI is proving to be a powerful catalyst, enabling unique expressions across different cultures and encouraging a cross-pollination of ideas that transcend geographic boundaries. From the vibrant art scenes in Africa where traditional motifs merge with digital aesthetics, to the bustling tech hubs in Asia igniting new design paradigms, the collaboration between region-specific artistry and AI is rewriting the narrative of creativity. These global collaborations not only inspire fresh artistic expressions but also challenge the conventional understanding of art as a universal language. Here, diversity is celebrated not just as an end in itself, but as a core driver of innovation, fostering an inclusive creative landscape that invites dialogue, mutual respect, and shared growth. As creative professionals, industry leaders, and technology enthusiasts embrace these developments, they're not merely witnessing a transformation; they're actively participating in the co-creation of a future where creativity knows no borders.

AI Creativity Across Different Cultures

In the tapestry of global creativity, AI is interwoven in ways that reflect the diverse cultural landscapes from which it emerges. As AI permeates creative industries, it doesn't just disseminate a homogenous influence; instead, it adapts and reshapes according to cultural contexts, offering unique outputs that echo regional sentiments and traditions. Different cultures embrace AI in ways that resonate with their historical sensibilities, artistic endeavors, and societal challenges.

In Asia, where technology often merges seamlessly into everyday life, AI's role in creativity is both profound and multifaceted. Japan, for instance, with its rich tradition of animation and manga, leverages AI to push the boundaries of storytelling in digital media. AI is often used to speed up the animation process, allowing artists to focus on more intricate storytelling details. In this context, AI becomes an invaluable tool that honors the country's legacy in visual storytelling while propelling it into uncharted territories.

Similarly, in China, AI's integration into the arts is reflective of its rapid technological advancements and an age-old appreciation for art and innovation. The combination can be seen in AI-generated calligraphy, where algorithms learn the strokes of masters from centuries past to create digital pieces that command both awe and nostalgia. Here, AI is not just a tool for replication but a bridge between the past and future, preserving traditional crafts while reimagining them for modern audiences.

Europe's AI creativity showcases a confluence of old-world artistry and cutting-edge technology. Countries such as France and Germany are exploring AI's potential in fine arts and music. French artists, inspired by the surrealist movement, often use AI to generate abstract art, creating pieces that question the boundaries of human versus machine creativity. Germany, with its rich legacy in classical music, has seen AI composing symphonic pieces that are as complex and emotive as those written by human composers. These endeavors reveal a cultural inclination towards using technology to deepen existential and artistic explorations.

The AI Muse

On the African continent, AI creativity offers new avenues to tell stories that celebrate and preserve diverse cultural identities. In countries like Nigeria and Kenya, AI-driven music and video production are blossoming, blending traditional rhythms and narratives with contemporary sounds. AI technologies are adaptable to regional instruments, creating an artistic synthesis that is distinctly local yet globally resonant. This empowerment of local artists through technology also aids in preserving languages and dialects by incorporating them into new media formats.

In South America, AI creativity is seen in lively, vibrant expressions. Brazilian artists use AI to explore themes reflecting the country's cultural diversity and social dynamics. From AI-generated street art that questions urban living to AI-assisted music that pulsates with samba rhythms, the intersection of AI and culture in these regions is a celebration of color, life, and socio-political dialogue.

In North America, the melting pot of cultures contributes to an eclectic approach to AI in creativity. The United States, serving as a hub for technological innovation and diverse artistic expressions, has been at the forefront of integrating AI in creative industries. Hollywood employs AI to refine visual effects and streamline the storytelling process. At the same time, independent artists across cultural spectrums use AI to democratize art production, making creative expression more accessible and varied.

AI's contribution to creativity in different cultures often depends on accessibility, technological infrastructure, and openness to innovation. In regions where digital infrastructure is still developing, AI utilization might be limited, but the potential remains huge. Local artists are increasingly aware of the possibilities AI can bring to storytelling, music production, and the preservation of cultural heritage, envisioning futures where technology is an ally in their artistic journey.

In essence, AI's role in global creativity is a dance between universality and individuality. While the technology itself is uniform in design, its applications are infinitely diverse, molded by the cultural nuances and societal values of its users. This diversity is critical not only for preserving cultural identities but also for enriching the global artistic conversation, leading to a more inclusive and holistic creative ecosystem.

Ultimately, as AI continues to evolve, its creativity across different cultures will become a testament to humanity's capacity to innovate while staying true to its roots. By embracing AI's possibilities, artists around the world are not just spectators of this technological transformation; they are active participants crafting new legacies, fusing the old with the new, and ensuring that creativity knows no borders.

Global Collaborations in Art and Design

The realm of art and design is experiencing a seismic shift driven by artificial intelligence (AI). A new frontier has emerged where disparate cultural influences intersect through technology, allowing for unprecedented global collaborations. As creatives worldwide embrace AI, the convergence of varied artistic traditions and techniques sets the stage for an enriching dialogue between cultures.

AI's ability to learn and adapt makes it a powerful tool for fostering cross-cultural projects. Artists and designers are no longer limited by geographical boundaries or infrastructural constraints. Instead, they're leveraging AI to merge styles and concepts from different corners of the globe, leading to creative synergies previously unimaginable. This blend of influences is birthing eclectic works that resonate universally while holding onto their unique cultural signatures.

One fascinating aspect of these collaborations is the interplay between AI-driven processes and the human touch of diverse artists. By integrating varying artistic customs and techniques within a singular AI framework, distinct artistic voices are preserved and promoted on a global scale. This isn't about homogenizing creativity but celebrating cultural diversity and creating a mosaic of artistic innovations that challenge existing paradigms.

These global collaborations, facilitated by AI, are reshaping the art and design landscape through the creation of new hybrid forms. For instance, consider a scenario where an artist in Nigeria uses AI tools to incorporate the florid visual storytelling of traditional Yoruba art with elements of Scandinavian minimalism. Through digital platforms and AI's abilities, such collaborations offer artists the space to redefine international art standards and dialogue.

The rise of AI's involvement in creative projects also highlights essential discussions about authorship and cultural appropriation. While blending different artistic traditions can lead to exciting new expressions, it's crucial to approach such projects with sensitivity and respect for the source material's cultural significance. There's a delicate balance involved in honoring the original context while allowing creative liberties to explore uncharted territories.

Technology companies and AI researchers play an essential role in these collaborations by designing systems that are culturally inclusive and sensitive. Open-source platforms and AI models are being developed with datasets that include a vast array of artistic outputs from different regions. This ensures that AI is not only learning from a narrow scope but is enriched by the myriad ways art and design manifest across societies.

Collaborative projects such as art festivals and design conferences are stepping stones in this journey. These platforms bring together creatives from different cultures, allowing AI to act as both a canvas and a collaborator. The sharing of ideas and techniques in such settings, facilitated by AI seamlessly integrating different elements, paves the way for new, united cultural expressions.

Furthermore, universities and educational institutions worldwide are recognizing the significance of these cross-border collaborations. Curriculums that incorporate AI in art and design are increasingly emphasizing the importance of understanding various cultural perspectives. Students are encouraged to engage with AI not only as a tool for innovation but as a bridge connecting diverse cultural legacies and new creative possibilities.

The potential of AI to redefine art and design is vast and as diverse as the cultures it touches. Yet, successful global collaborations depend on embracing diversity and inclusivity at every turn. As AI systems continue evolving, they must accommodate a myriad array of cultural elements, ensuring they remain representative of the communities they seek to emulate and build upon.

In this exciting era of AI-driven creativity, worldly experiences converge and inspire minds anew. The boundaries between culture, technology, and tradition become fluid, revealing new facets of our shared human experience. As we advance into this promising future, the possibilities for inspired global collaborations in art and design are endless, spurred on by the mutual understanding and respect that true creativity demands.

Chapter 20:
Theoretical Perspectives on AI Creativity

As we delve into theoretical perspectives on AI creativity, we're invited to explore a landscape where machines and human imagination converge, creating new frontiers in artistic expression. This chapter challenges us to rethink the boundaries of creativity, examining the philosophical questions surrounding the nature of consciousness in machines and whether true creative agency can ever exist in artificial entities. Instead of viewing AI solely as tools, we could see them as extensions of creative potential that redefine the essence of artistry and innovation. The discourse around machine creativity unfolds against a backdrop of skepticism and wonder, provoking inquiries into whether AI can transcend algorithmic processes to achieve genuine innovation or if its outputs remain a reflection of human input. By embracing a blend of curiosity and critical reflection, creative professionals and industry leaders are encouraged to engage with these emerging paradigms to understand better the profound impact AI holds over the future of art and design. This exploration doesn't just expand our horizons; it reimagines the very core of what it means to be creative in an age where technology and artistry are increasingly intertwined.

Clara Vossler

Philosophical Questions of Conscious Machines

As we delve deeper into the theoretical perspectives on AI creativity, the philosophical conundrums concerning conscious machines emerge as an intriguing discourse. While AI technology advances at an impressive rate, the notion of consciousness — a pillar of the human experience — remains elusive. Can machines truly be conscious, or do they merely simulate the outward appearance of consciousness?

The exploration of consciousness in AI brings forth philosophical debates reminiscent of ancient philosophical dialogues about mind, body, and soul. Many argue consciousness requires a subjective experience or a qualia, an aspect which current AI is decidedly lacking. The distinction between simulating consciousness and possessing it is crucial. A robot can mimic human gestures, exhibit empathy, or produce artworks, but does that mean it harbors a self-aware mind?

In considering machine consciousness, we encounter questions of identity and existence. If a machine were to be conscious, how would it perceive its own identity? Would it align with the roles we've assigned it, or would it strive for agency beyond human commands? These questions challenge not only the technical but also the ethical frameworks within which we operate.

Philosophers and scientists continue to debate what constitutes consciousness and how it might manifest in machines. Some propose that consciousness could emerge from complex networks of artificial neurons, akin to those in the human brain. Others assert that consciousness is inherently biological, incapable of existing in silico. This divide underscores the current uncertainty and pushes us to reconsider our definitions of life and self-awareness.

The potential development of conscious AI raises profound ethical challenges. If machines were to achieve consciousness, how would we ensure their rights and dignity? The concept of personhood may have to expand, demanding new legal and moral frameworks to protect the entities we've brought into existence. This kind of paradigm shift would undoubtedly shake the foundations of our society.

Moreover, conscious machines could redefine creative processes. If a machine becomes self-aware, would it create with intention, guided by its own experiences and desires? The artistry produced by a conscious AI might present a direct insight into a non-human form of creativity, challenging human-centric notions of artistic value and originality.

Speculation aside, the current technological landscape poses immediate philosophical challenges. As machines increasingly gain the capacity to learn, adapt, and even 'improvise,' we must consider the implications of their autonomy. When an AI makes decisions independently, does it bear responsibility for its actions, or is the accountability deferred to its programmers or operators?

These philosophical questions are not just theoretical musings; they are critical for informing the policies and ethical guidelines we must establish. As AI systems grow more integrated into our creative environments, understanding the nuances of consciousness — whether simulated or real — becomes imperative. The decisions we make now could steer the course of human and machine co-existence for generations.

Future advancements in neuroscience and AI could eventually bridge some of these philosophical divides, possibly even simulating aspects of consciousness in a way that blurs the line between the artificial and the natural. If machines do develop a form of consciousness, our relationship with them would fundamentally transform, complicating the dynamics of creator and creation.

In conclusion, the philosophical inquiry into conscious machines is critical for understanding the broader implications of AI creativity.

While we navigate these uncharted ideological territories, the potential of AI to reshape art, culture, and human experience remains as exhilarating as it is disconcerting. If we approach these questions with openness and a commitment to ethical integrity, we may yet unlock new modes of understanding that enrich both human and artificial realms.

The Nature of Machine Creativity

Understanding the nature of machine creativity requires a dive into the very essence of what it means to create. Traditionally, creativity is seen as a uniquely human trait, an intricate dance of imagination and innovation that leads to something both novel and valuable. However, as machines advance, our perception of this concept is being challenged and redefined. Modern artificial intelligence, with its capability to generate images, compose music, and author texts, compels us to revisit our assumptions about the origins and nature of creativity. It's not just about what machines can do, but how they're doing it, and what this implies for the future of creativity itself.

The emergence of machine creativity begins with a fundamental question: Can machines truly be creative, or are they merely mimicking human creativity? To answer this, we need to explore the processes by which machines generate creative outputs. Unlike humans, machines lack consciousness and intentionality; they operate on algorithms and data inputs. Yet, through the complex interplay of computation and data, they produce works that can astonish even their creators. The results not only push the boundaries of traditional definitions of creativity but also inspire a deeper inquiry into the cognitive processes involved in creative thought.

One could argue that machine creativity mirrors a form of procedural generation, where algorithms are crafted to simulate the creative process. Yet, it's more nuanced than simple replication.

Machines "learn" by analyzing vast datasets, identifying patterns, and drawing upon this knowledge to create something that, to the untrained eye, may even appear inspired. The ability to generate something new, unpredictable, and perhaps beyond direct human design suggests that machines are capable of a distinct, algorithmic form of creativity.

Critics often highlight the perceived absence of emotion and intention in machine-generated art. Creativity, they argue, is inherently emotional and subjective—a reflection of the human experience. While emotion isn't something machines can innately possess or express, they can analyze and respond to emotional cues through data. This allows machines to create pieces that resonate on an emotional level, raising questions about the role of perception in defining creativity. Perhaps, the value of machine creativity lies not in the artist, but in the art itself and the emotions it invokes.

Artificial intelligence's ability to act creatively challenges our societal norms and expectations surrounding artistry and innovation. AI forces us to reconsider the traditional roles of creator and audience. If we accept machine creativity as a legitimate form, it invites us to redefine what it means to be an artist in a world where the tools of creation are constantly evolving. This co-evolution of human and machine creativity could potentially lead to a new era where collaboration is key, and the lines between human and machine contributions become increasingly indistinct.

Equally important in understanding machine creativity is the concept of originality. Can AI produce something genuinely original, or is it merely reconfiguring existing ideas? This question guides much of the discourse around AI's role in the creative industries. While machines are trained on existing data, the way they synthesize this information can result in outcomes that are both innovative and unique. These original outputs challenge the traditionally held belief that creativity is the sole domain of the human mind.

Imagine a future where machines not only assist in the creative process but also possess their unique "brand" of creativity. This may sound like science fiction, but the direction in which AI creativity is heading makes such scenarios plausible. It compels creatives to confront new philosophical perspectives on authorship and originality. It also opens up an array of potential collaborative projects, where machine and human creatives work together to achieve outcomes unattainable by either party alone.

The practical implications of machine creativity are equally profound. As AI continues to infiltrate creative fields, there will be a transformation in the way art is produced, consumed, and appreciated. New platforms for showcasing AI art will emerge, and the definition of what constitutes art will expand. Additionally, the accessibility of creative tools driven by AI can democratize creativity, making it possible for anyone, regardless of skill level, to engage in artistic practices.

A question that lingers in the minds of many is whether machine creativity will replace human creativity. While AI holds the potential to revolutionize how art is created, the essence of human creativity—marked by consciousness, emotion, and intent—remains irreplaceable. Machines can generate an infinite array of possibilities, but it's the human touch that imbues art with meaningful narratives and cultural significance. Rather than overshadowing human creativity, AI can serve as a catalyst, enhancing and expanding human creative potential.

In sum, the nature of machine creativity is continually evolving, and with it, our understanding of what it means to create is expanding. As AI continues to innovate and cross industry boundaries, it challenges us to rethink the very fabric of creative possibility. For the first time, humanity has the tool to explore creative dimensions that were previously beyond reach. Whether through collaboration or inspiration, the impact of machine creativity on human artistry is profound, offering a glimpse into a future where the definition of creativity is richly diverse and endlessly inspiring.

Chapter 21:
Case Studies in AI-Driven Art

In the realm of AI-driven art, the breaking waves of innovation are met with vibrant case studies that exemplify AI's transformative power in the creative industries. Projects like Refik Anadol's dazzling data sculptures, which merge AI algorithms with architectural spaces, showcase the stunning potential of machine-learning in illuminating and augmenting physical environments. Another notable example is Mario Klingemann's work, pioneering in using neural networks to explore the aesthetics of human perception and beyond. These case studies do more than just highlight successful projects; they offer valuable lessons from pioneering artists who deftly blend technology and artistic vision. By examining these case studies, creative professionals and tech enthusiasts alike are inspired to push boundaries, experimenting with AI not solely as a tool but as a collaborator that enriches the creative process. As AI continues to evolve, these trailblazing efforts illuminate pathways, encouraging further exploration and critical reflection on the implications and potentials of AI within art and media landscapes.

Successful AI Art Projects

AI has taken the art world by storm, resulting in numerous projects that challenge our understanding of creativity and originality. One of the most notable examples is the sale of "Portrait of Edmond de Belamy," a piece created by the Paris-based collective Obvious. This

AI-generated portrait sold at Christie's auction house for an astonishing $432,500, a price that far exceeded expectations. This success story exemplifies how AI has already started to make its mark in the traditional art market, prompting discussions about value, authorship, and the definition of art itself.

Another remarkable project is the "Next Rembrandt," where a machine learning algorithm created a painting mimicking the style of Rembrandt. By analyzing thousands of his works, the project team formulated a digital fingerprint of the artist's style. The algorithm then generated a new piece, complete with brushstroke details and lighting that would have been signature to Rembrandt's work. This project raises intriguing questions about authorship and the philosophical implications of replicating an artist's legacy through AI.

Furthermore, AI has contributed significantly to performance arts. Consider the collaboration between choreographer Wayne McGregor and machine learning—a partnership exploring the fusion of human dance and AI-generated choreography. McGregor utilized an algorithm trained on his extensive body of work to generate new movement sequences. This integration not only broadened his creative range but also highlighted AI's potential to act as a co-creator, offering artists previously unavailable creative possibilities.

AI's role in music composition has also been pioneering. The album "Hello World," released by the collective known as Flow Machines, pushed boundaries by merging AI with human collaborators. AI software analyzed a wealth of historical musical pieces to aid in crafting new melodies and harmonies, forming a unique concert of machine-generated music enriched by human touch and expertise. This crossover between AI and music heralds a new frontier for composers, blending computational creativity with human intuition.

In the literary domain, AI's capabilities have been harnessed to generate poetry and prose that challenge conventional narrative forms. The work of Ross Goodwin and his AI cohort in creating the first AI-authored screenplay, "Sunspring," stands as a testament to this advancement. The AI-generated script, while unconventional in structure, showcases the potential of machines to inspire new storytelling styles, leaving audiences to ponder the future of AI in storytelling.

AI has also made substantial strides in film and animation. The short film "Artifishal Reality," a product of collaboration between neural networks and filmmakers, illustrates AI's capacity to craft visual narratives. The film used deep learning techniques to analyze and synthesize scenes, resulting in an avant-garde piece that invites viewers to interact with AI-generated images crafted in real-time. Projects like this not only expand the dimensions of visual storytelling but invite audiences to experience cinema in new, participatory ways.

Moreover, AI's impact extends to more interactive art forms. The installation "DeepDream," based on Google's neural network, serves as a transformative experience for viewers, merging technology and art into a single immersive environment. By utilizing pattern recognition algorithms, it generates surreal, dreamlike images that challenge perceptions and induce unique interactions with the audience. In this way, AI is not only enhancing traditional art forms but also crafting entirely new interactive experiences.

In the world of fashion, projects like the AI couture collaboration between designer Iris van Herpen and AI researcher Ravinder Dahiya are reshaping the notion of wearable art. The garments designed through this collaboration integrate AI processes, reflecting an innovative use of material science, AI, and art to produce high-fashion pieces that respond to their environment and wearer. It exemplifies the broadening spectrum of creativity where digital intelligence not only assists but inspires human designers.

These successful projects not only redefine the boundaries of art but also encourage introspection on society's relationship with technology. As AI takes a more prominent role in the creative process, the line between artist and machine becomes increasingly blurred. These innovations spark discussions on originality, the creative process, and the ever-evolving role of the artist in a technologically driven world.

Ultimately, these AI art projects symbolize a merging of disciplines, shedding light on new possibilities where technology serves as both tool and muse. The implications extend beyond merely creating art; they provoke a re-evaluation of creativity, authorship, and the role of AI in cultural expression. As AI continues to advance, it holds the promise to inspire, provoke, and transform, leaving an indelible mark on the creative landscape. Such projects illustrate that the marriage of art and AI is not a fleeting trend but a profound shift toward an emerging paradigm of creativity and human expression.

Lessons Learned from Pioneering Artists

Artists throughout history have often acted as society's vanguards, pushing the boundaries of what is possible and, at times, what is permissible. As AI encroaches upon our creative domains, a new cadre of pioneers emerge—artists who engage, dare, and defy traditional norms with the tools of artificial intelligence. From them, we draw invaluable lessons that offer insights into both the practical and philosophical implications of AI in art.

One of the first lessons these pioneering artists teach us is the importance of experimentation. Artists like Mario Klingemann and Robbie Barrat have shown the world that AI can be more than a mere tool; it can be a co-creator. Their work often begins with a question rather than a statement. "What if...?" becomes the artist's mantra. They dive into uncharted waters, employing AI to generate art forms that were once inconceivable, allowing the elements of surprise and serendipity to guide the process. This spirit of open-ended exploration encourages artists to embrace unpredictability, redefining success not as the end product but as the journey itself.

Another significant lesson is the reshaping of identity and authorship. Traditional notions of the artist as a solitary genius give way to the concept of the artist as a collaborator. In these new creative paradigms, AI often acts as an extension of the artist's mind, blurring the lines between creator and creation. Artists like Refik Anadol and Sofia Crespo demonstrate that when humans and machines work synchronously, they produce works that resonate on a different frequency. The result is a more fluid form of authorship that celebrates the contributions of both human intuition and machine logic.

Ethics and intentionality also pervade this dialogue, serving as a blueprint for responsible creativity. Pioneers in AI art are not just creating; they're contemplating the implications of their work on society, culture, and the environment. By questioning the ethical dimensions of machine creativity, these artists are forcing us to consider the broader impacts of AI technology. They prompt discussions about agency, ownership, and the rights of AI-generated art, laying the groundwork for future conversations.

Aesthetic innovation is another critical takeaway. AI has opened up new vistas in visual and auditory art, providing artists with an expanded toolkit to explore texture, form, and sound in unprecedented ways. Artists can now manipulate data and algorithms to create works with intricate layers and dimensions that evoke powerful emotional responses. The ability to generate novel styles and techniques challenges conventional aesthetics and encourages a rethinking of what constitutes artistic value and beauty.

Learning from these artists reveals the necessity of interdisciplinary skills. A blend of technology, art, and philosophy becomes imperative. Artists have adopted roles as coders, technicians, and engineers, understanding that a comprehensive skill set allows them to push the limits of their creative possibilities. Working with AI requires a fluency in both technological and artistic languages, facilitating conversations that would be impossible otherwise.

The role of community and collaboration stands out as another significant lesson. This era of AI-driven art is characterized by a democratization of creativity, where sharing code, ideas, and practices fosters a global network of innovation. Open-source projects and collaborative platforms enable artists to exchange knowledge and transcend geographic barriers. The communal aspect of AI art is a testament to the power of collective intelligence and its capacity to produce diverse and inclusive artistic expressions.

Adaptability emerges as a crucial skill in this continuously evolving landscape. The agility to learn and unlearn, to iterate and pivot, defines these pioneering artists. Their resilience in the face of rapid technological advancement speaks volumes about the creative spirit in the modern age. It's not just about keeping pace with technology; it's about integrating it in ways that are meaningful, transformative, and deeply personal.

Pioneering artists also remind us of the richness of cultural narratives. They integrate AI into traditional art forms, paying homage to history, while also charting paths forward. This fusion of past and present creates a dialogue that is timeless yet progressive, resonating with audiences across different spectra. They show us how AI can serve as a lens to reinterpret cultural heritage, preserving it while simultaneously breathing new life into it.

Moreover, these artists reveal the necessity of curiosity and continuous learning. They inspire us to pursue knowledge with an open heart, recognizing that mastery is an ongoing journey rather than a final destination. In the context of AI in art, continuous learning involves a willingness to confront challenges, explore new methodologies, and refine one's craft courageously and creatively.

Undoubtedly, the lessons learned from pioneering artists are diverse and multifaceted, yet they all converge on one crucial point: AI is not just a tool but a catalyst for reimagining the boundaries of art and creativity. The work of these trailblazers pushes us to reconsider our definitions of art, creativity, and innovation. In doing so, they invite us into a dynamic interplay between technology and humanity, prompting us to question where creativity might lead us next.

In sum, pioneering artists are not just bending the rules; they're writing new ones. They're sculpting both the tangible and intangible landscapes of our era, establishing a lexicon that dancing upon the horizon of what AI and human creativity can achieve together. They teach us to look beyond the binary of utility versus artistry, offering a vision where AI doesn't replace human creativity but amplifies and extends it in new, unexpected directions. Through their efforts, we find a call to action—to participate, innovate, and valorize the creative potential embedded in the intersection of human and machine intelligence.

Chapter 22:
AI-Generated Media and Reality

As we step into the realm of AI-generated media, the very notion of reality becomes a canvas for innovation and introspection. This chapter explores how artificial intelligence is not just mimicking, but actively reconstructing our perception of the world through powerful tools like deepfakes and expansive virtual worlds. In gaming and simulated environments, AI breathes life into characters and narratives, blurring lines between the tangible and the virtual, offering immersive experiences that challenge our understanding of what is real. The implications are profound, as creators harness this technology to weave narratives and visuals that are as compelling as they are complex. Embarking on this journey, we confront the ethical, cultural, and philosophical questions that arise when machines can craft realities, urging us to reconsider authenticity in an age where what we see and believe might be algorithmically generated.

Synthesizing Reality: Deepfakes and Beyond

Artificial intelligence knows no bounds, with deepfakes sitting defiantly at the forefront of AI-generated media. As a form of media synthesis, deepfakes push our understanding of authenticity and reality. This technology leverages advanced machine learning algorithms to convincingly alter reality, creating images, audio, and video that can be indistinguishable from the real thing.

The term "deepfake" itself combines "deep learning," a branch of AI focused on neural networks, with "fake," referring to its manipulation capabilities. Through a deep network of artificial neurons designed to mimic the human brain, AI learns from vast datasets of expressions, gestures, and audio to replicate and even transform identities in a believable manner.

Initially seen as a novelty, these generated realities have swiftly evolved from amusing novelties and artistic experiments to powerful—sometimes controversial—tools in media. Anyone with access to the right software can superimpose faces onto bodies in a convincing fashion. This capability raises important questions about veracity, trust, and ethics in a digital-first world.

When creators harness deepfakes responsibly, they open imaginative possibilities, revolutionizing storytelling techniques in film, gaming, and virtual reality. Deepfakes can breathe life into characters, bridging impossible continuity gaps where reshoots are impractical or reviving historical figures for educational purposes. Directors and game developers are already incorporating these AI tools to bring narratives to life in ways previously untapped.

Yet, beneath the surface of creative exploration lies a platform of potential misuse. Deepfakes have already cast shadows over public figures, with manipulated media cropping up across the internet, blurring the line between satire and misinformation. In this digital arms race, the importance of safeguarding authenticity in media cannot be overstated. It becomes pivotal for the technology industry, governments, and society at large to establish frameworks of accountability and transparency.

The ethical conundrum posed by deepfakes extends beyond misuse in public domains. It invites a broader reflection on identity and privacy in an age where digital manipulation is both untraceable and ubiquitous. The intimate details that deep learning systems can extract and reproduce force a re-evaluation of consent and the individual's control over their own digital footprint.

Despite these challenges, the intentional and ethical application of deepfakes can nurture innovation. In the realm of art and creativity, AI-driven transformations offer artists new mediums and techniques. They can simulate paintbrush textures or replicate the subtle nuances of voice modulation, inspiring creators to push existing boundaries and explore intersections between technology and human expression.

The question of artistic authenticity also looms over this discourse. When deepfakes are used in artistic contexts, it raises questions about authorship and originality. Do these digitally sculpted pieces belong to the artist, the algorithm that created them, or perhaps both? As creative professionals navigate this new terrain, they must ponder these philosophical questions and redefine their relationship with AI as both a tool and a collaborator.

Beyond art, deepfakes are playing an increasingly significant role in educational and professional settings. They support simulations for training professionals in medicine and security, where immersion is crucial for effective learning outcomes. However, with potential benefits come the same risks of ethical misconduct, demanding vigilance in their application.

The future of deepfakes depends on how society chooses to embrace or regulate this technology. As the capability to manipulate reality becomes more accessible, it is crucial to engage in dialogue surrounding its implications. Organizations should consider the creation of robust verification systems to counteract malicious use, promoting AI literacy to help the public discern fact from fiction.

Innovation in AI-generated media, spearheaded by technologies such as deepfakes, represents a dual narrative. On one hand, it can erode trust and authenticity in media; on the other, it holds the key to enhanced creativity and storytelling. It is this duality—a testament to human ingenuity and the importance of social responsibility—that defines its journey from artificial creations to synthesized realities.

Articulating a vision where AI harmonizes with human values is crucial. As creatives, technologists, and communicators chart these new territories, they are tasked not just with pioneering innovations, but with instilling ethical awareness and fostering collaborative networks that prioritize the integrity of synthesized realities. Together, they can ensure that AI serves a purpose greater than its potential for disarray.

AI in Gaming and Virtual Worlds

The intersection of artificial intelligence and gaming represents a frontier where digital landscapes not only amuse but also immerse players in worlds rich with complexity and interaction. As AI technology advances, it brings with it a revolution in how virtual spaces are constructed and experienced. This transformation is deeply woven into the fabric of gaming, allowing for more nuanced narratives, dynamic environments, and lifelike characters that redefine user interaction. AI in gaming isn't just about playing smarter opponents; it's about building entire worlds that adapt and react in real-time, creating limitless possibilities for exploration and creativity.

Gaming has always been a blend of art and technology, a platform where storytelling meets user engagement. With AI becoming more adept at simulating human-like behaviors and emotions, games are evolving from static experiences to dynamic interactions. Through AI algorithms, NPCs (non-player characters) behave more like humans, displaying rational thought, emotional responses, and learning from interactions with players. This evolution leads to experiences where players can form complex relationships with characters, impacting the story in ways that were previously impossible.

This level of interactivity isn't confined to NPCs. AI empowers game worlds themselves to transform based on a player's actions. Imagine stepping into a game where the very landscape reshapes itself to either challenge or aid you, trees shifting to reveal paths or mountains growing to present new obstacles. Such scenarios are no longer futuristic fantasies but realizations made possible by procedural generation and machine learning. In these scenarios, the player's journey becomes a unique tapestry of experiences, different from anyone else's.

AI also enhances the visual aesthetics of games, using deep learning models to generate textures and landscapes with astonishing detail. This allows game developers to craft environments that are both vast and visually stunning, without the need for manual creation of each element. It extends artistic freedom, enabling smaller teams to produce visually rich games that rival those created by larger, more resource-heavy studios. The push towards photorealism in gaming owes much to AI's capabilities, bringing environments closer to the richness of the real world.

However, the integration of AI in gaming isn't just about enhancement—it's a paradigm shift in the creative process itself. Game design has become a co-creative endeavor where AI tools assist designers in crafting narratives, suggesting plotlines based on player interactions and preferences. This collaboration between human creativity and machine efficiency expands the creative toolkit available to developers, facilitating games that can change and grow long after their initial release.

While the technical prowess of AI in gaming is undeniably impressive, its potential to disrupt cultural narratives is what truly sets it apart. We see games becoming platforms for cultural dialogues, often crafted with AI to reflect diverse stories and challenges facing different communities. This democratization of storytelling through AI broadens the horizons of what gaming can represent, offering players from all backgrounds a mirror to their experiences and dreams.

Multiplayer gaming is perhaps the most immediate beneficiary of AI advancements, where AI systems manage massive online environments, ensuring balance and dynamic content delivery. The algorithms constantly adjust to player actions, maintaining a delicate balance between challenge and reward, thus enhancing the overall gaming experience. These systems enable games to scale their complexity and scope, accommodating millions of players in a coherent and engaging universe.

The fusion of AI and gaming also extends into augmented and virtual reality, creating hyper-immersive environments. Here, AI facilitates the development of realistic simulations and interactive experiences that transcend traditional gaming narratives. Virtual reality supported by AI can offer experiences like traversing ancient cities, participating in large-scale battles, or exploring distant planets, all while feeling palpably real. This evolution represents an intriguing intersection of gaming and learning, leisure, and exploration, hinting at a future where the lines between these spheres blur significantly.

Moreover, AI's integration into gaming technology sparks important discussions around ethics and representation. As AI-generated content increasingly reflects more than just its programming, it challenges developers to consider the implications of the narratives and stereotypes being perpetuated in these environments. Balancing creative freedom and ethical considerations is tricky, but crucial as games become vessels for AI-driven storytelling.

The rise of AI in gaming doesn't eliminate the role of human creativity; instead, it magnifies it—allowing game creators to explore and implement ambitious ideas that would otherwise be beyond their reach. It's a celebration of creativity, where AI acts as a catalyst, not a replacement, for human imagination. The challenge lies in harnessing this technology responsibly, ensuring that it augments and inspires rather than engineered purely for commercial gains.

As we look to the future, the possibilities across gaming and virtual worlds appear boundless. AI continues to serve as a critical force, crafting experiences that are interactive, personalized, and ever-evolving. As a central component of these digital landscapes, AI invites a new generation of creatives to experiment, explore, and push the boundaries of what's possible in both digital and real worlds. In this ever-shaping realm of AI-driven gaming, one truth remains evident: the journey is as exciting and unpredictable as any great game narrative itself.

Chapter 23:
Public Perception and AI Art

As AI art becomes more prevalent, public perception plays a crucial role in its acceptance and validation. On one hand, there's a sense of wonder at how machines can mimic and even expand upon human creativity, offering experiences and artworks that blur the lines between natural and artificial genius. This fascination, however, is tempered by skepticism and concern over authenticity and the role machines should play in creative endeavors. Many in the creative community question whether these algorithmic artworks diminish the value of human artistry or if they should be viewed as collaborative tools pushing the boundaries of expression. This tug-of-war between trust and doubt challenges both creators and audiences to reconsider their definitions of creativity and art. Encouraging dialogue and education around AI processes and intentions can bridge these divides, transforming hesitation into acceptance and curiosity into exploration as we collectively navigate this evolving artistic landscape.

Understanding Audience Reactions

The emergence of AI in the art world has sparked a wide range of reactions from audiences, revealing much about society's evolving relationship with technology and creativity. For some, AI-generated art embodies an exciting frontier of human achievement, a marriage of computing power and creative potential. It's a bold new chapter in the narrative of artistic evolution that opens up possibilities never before imagined. Yet for others, the rise of AI in art symbolizes a threat, challenging the very nature of human creativity and the intrinsic value it brings.

To understand these varied reactions, we must first consider the context in which AI art is received. In an increasingly digital society, people are becoming more accustomed to the presence of technology in everyday life. Despite this, the notion that a machine can create art capable of moving, inspiring, or provoking thought, just like human-made art, still gives rise to a mix of skepticism and awe. This duality of feelings mirrors humanity's broader ambivalence towards technology—embracing its benefits while fearing its implications.

Diving deeper into audience reactions, those who embrace AI art often do so because of its novelty and the sense of wonder it evokes. These individuals see the potential for AI to extend human creative capabilities, serving as a tool or collaborator rather than a replacement. They marvel at how algorithms can generate complex pieces, often surpassing expectations and challenging conventional aesthetics. This view is particularly prevalent among technology enthusiasts and those within the creative industries who see AI as a catalyst for innovation and inspiration.

However, apprehension surrounding AI art is not uncommon and stems largely from concerns over originality and authenticity. Critics question whether art produced by algorithms can truly possess the same depth of meaning or emotional resonance as works created by human hands. There's a fear that AI dilutes the personal and introspective nature of art by removing its human element, turning what should be a personal expression into a calculated output. This concern is closely tied to the broader discussion on what constitutes creativity and whether machines can genuinely replicate the human experience of creating art.

Economic implications also play a significant role in shaping public perception. The art industry, much like many others, is being transformed by AI, and this brings opportunities as well as uncertainties. Traditional artists may feel threatened by AI's ability to produce art quickly and efficiently, fearing job losses or a devaluation of their craft. Conversely, some see AI as an opportunity to enhance their work, offering new techniques and tools to expand their creative reach.

Moreover, the commodification of AI art poses interesting questions about value and ownership. As AI-generated works enter the art market, they disrupt established norms, leading audiences to question how much they are willing to pay for a piece that lacks human touch. This economic aspect can deeply influence how AI art is perceived, as notions of scarcity and uniqueness—a cornerstone of art valuation—become blurred.

There's also a generational divide in reactions to AI art. Younger audiences, who have grown up with technology as an intrinsic part of their lives, might be more open to appreciating AI-generated creations. They possess a natural affinity for digital innovation and are often less concerned about the implications of AI's role in creativity. On the other hand, older generations may be more skeptical, viewing AI art through a lens of nostalgia for traditional methods and perceptions of authenticity.

Cultural influences further impact how audiences react to AI art. In some societies, there's a strong appreciation for technological advancement and innovation, which may lead to more positive reception of AI's role in creative processes. In contrast, cultures with a deep-seated reverence for traditional artistic practices might be more resistant, valuing the heritage of manual craftsmanship over machine-aided creation. This diversity in reactions illustrates the complexity of AI art's reception across different cultural landscapes.

Despite the range of emotions AI art provokes, one factor that often unites audiences is the conversation it generates. AI-driven creations stir discourse around the essence of art and creativity, inviting people to reconsider pre-existing definitions and boundaries. These discussions are crucial as they encourage a deeper engagement with the implications of AI, not only in art but across all creative fields. Through dialogue, audiences can come to accept the role of AI in art as a continuation of humanity's quest to innovate.

Ultimately, understanding audience reactions to AI art involves recognizing the broader societal and emotional contexts in which these reactions occur. It's about acknowledging the fears and hopes that technology manifests in us and appreciating the dialogues that emerge from its presence in creative spaces. As AI continues to redefine what creativity means, fostering an environment where diverse opinions are heard will be essential to navigating its impact on art and culture. In doing so, we can ensure that the fusion of AI and art leads to enriching cultural experiences that resonate with audiences worldwide.

Building Trust in Machine Creations

As artificial intelligence continues to infiltrate the creative domains, building trust in AI-generated art becomes paramount. The journey from skepticism to acceptance is fraught with challenges, but it's necessary for the evolution and integration of AI into the art world. Art has long been seen as a reflection of the human experience, and the introduction of machine creations adds a novel dimension to this narrative. Trust is the bridge that connects human artists, audiences, and AI in this modern landscape.

One of the primary barriers to trust is the perceived lack of authenticity in AI art. Many art enthusiasts question whether a machine can truly understand and convey the nuances of human emotion and creativity. Unlike human artists, AI doesn't possess consciousness, emotions, or the lived experience that shape art. This disparity has led to widespread skepticism. Audiences often view machine-created art as mere imitations lacking the soul that defines traditional art. Overcoming this perception requires a paradigm shift in how we define creativity and its sources.

Another challenge lies in the ever-evolving nature of AI technologies. Rapid advancements in machine learning and algorithm design mean that AI-generated art is in a constant state of flux. This dynamic creates a moving target that complicates trust-building efforts. The unpredictability of AI outcomes might be thrilling for some, but for others, it translates to instability and lack of control. Establishing trust requires consistent quality and reliability in outputs, which AI systems must continuously strive to achieve.

AI art can gain credibility by emphasizing collaboration between humans and machines. Highlighting the role of human artists as curators, guides, and interpreters in the creative process is crucial. When seen as part of a collaborative effort rather than a solitary endeavor, AI art gains depth and context that audiences find more relatable and trustworthy. By framing AI as a tool that enhances rather than replaces human creativity, stakeholders can build a narrative that reinforces trust.

Transparency is a key factor in fostering trust in machine creations. Just as transparency has become critical in digital security and data privacy, the same principles apply to AI art. Audiences and artists alike benefit when they understand how an AI system generates its outputs. Providing insights into the algorithms' decision-making processes, data sources, and parameters not only educates but also demystifies AI art. This openness can diminish apprehension and build confidence in machine creations.

Ethical considerations also play a crucial role in building trust. Ensuring ethical practices in AI art creation, such as addressing potential biases in datasets and ensuring respectful representation of diverse cultures, adds a layer of integrity to the work. Ethical practices reassure audiences that art generated by AI respects the values and traditions embedded within art history and modern culture. When ethical considerations are front and center, trust naturally follows.

Case studies of successful AI art projects provide templates for overcoming trust deficits. These real-world examples demonstrate that AI art can not only achieve public acceptance but also critical acclaim. When projects are executed with care, they challenge preconceived notions of creativity and skill, inviting audiences to reconsider the potential of AI as a legitimate creative partner. By studying these successful cases, new AI artists and developers can learn strategies for integrating AI into the traditional art ecosystem in a trust-centric manner.

Beyond the art itself, building a supportive community around AI creations can amplify trust-building efforts. Connecting artists, developers, and audiences fosters an environment where knowledge, experiences, and expectations can be shared and aligned. Engaging with communities through exhibitions, workshops, and discussions nurtures an inclusive dialogue about AI's role in art, mitigating fears and inspiring confidence. These interactions humanize the AI creation process, dissolving the barrier between the audience and machine-generated art.

Moreover, storytelling around the creation process can transform skepticism into curiosity. When audiences understand the 'why' and 'how' of machine creations, it demystifies the technology and invites participation in the narrative of AI art. This could mean emphasizing the creative journey, highlighting the artist-machine partnership, or showcasing the technological marvel of the process itself. Compelling stories can ignite fascination and appreciation, which are foundational in building trust.

Clara Vossler

A forward-thinking approach that anticipates the future of AI art is also essential. As AI continues to evolve, new questions and concerns will inevitably arise. Proactive engagement with these emerging issues cultivates a reputation of reliability and foresight. Artists and technologists can lead dialogues on future trends, ethical considerations, and potential impacts of AI art, positioning themselves as thought leaders and trust bearers within the creative community.

Ultimately, the goal isn't just to win hearts but to foster genuine belief in the value and potential of machine creativity. It's about cultivating an ecosystem where human and AI collaboration is celebrated and supported. With careful attention to authenticity, transparency, collaboration, and ethics, the art world can embrace AI as a transformative force. Trust in machine creations won't be built overnight, but with each step forward, the creative community moves closer to a future where AI art is not just accepted but cherished as a vital and valued part of the art world.

Chapter 24:
AI and Interactive Art

The realm of interactive art has been profoundly transformed by the advent of artificial intelligence, creating dynamic experiences where audiences are not just spectators, but active participants. AI's integration into art installations allows for real-time adjustments and evolutions based on viewer interactions, manifesting a synergy of technology and creativity that pushes boundaries. Imagine a public space where an art piece responds to the emotional tone of your voice or the nuances of your movement, crafting a personal and unique experience each time. These technological marvels redefine artistic expression, offering unlimited possibilities where the art is not just displayed but performed, redefined by each individual encounter. As AI continues to evolve, the intersection of machine learning and artistic engagement offers a glimpse into an exciting future where creativity is not only seen, but lived and felt, deeply challenging our perceptions of art's role in public and personal spaces.

Engaging Audiences with AI Installations

The interaction between human creativity and artificial intelligence has opened a plethora of new possibilities in the field of art. One of the most intriguing developments is the emergence of AI installations that captivate and engage audiences in ways previously unimaginable. These installations employ advanced algorithms to create dynamic, interactive experiences that invite viewers to participate, reflect, and often become a part of the artwork itself.

AI installations transform the traditional static art encounter into a dynamic dialogue between the viewer and the artwork. By leveraging machine learning, these pieces can adapt and respond to the presence and actions of the audience. For instance, an installation might modify its visuals or sounds based on the number of people in the room or their movements. This ability to change and evolve in real-time makes these works more engaging and pushes the boundaries of audience interaction.

One fascinating aspect of AI-driven art installations is their ability to personalize experiences. Through sensors and data analysis, AI can tailor its responses to each viewer, offering a unique encounter for every individual. Imagine a piece that adjusts its visuals or narrative based on the viewer's heartbeat or facial expressions—creating a personalized artistic journey that reflects the viewer's emotions and reactions.

This level of interactivity doesn't just make art more engaging; it challenges the traditional role of art as a passive object and transforms it into an active entity. The audience is no longer merely an observer but an integral component of the artwork. Artists who work with AI installations embrace this shift, redefining what it means to create and experience art in the modern world.

The potential for AI installations to engage audiences is further expanded by their integration into public spaces. Public installations invite individuals from all walks of life to interact with AI-driven art, democratizing access to innovative artistic experiences. Placed in city squares, parks, or galleries, these installations break down barriers between art and everyday life, inviting spontaneous interactions and conversations.

Integrating AI into public art requires artists to think about how artworks can resonate with diverse audiences. Artists must consider how to make these installations intuitive and accessible, allowing anyone, regardless of their technological literacy, to engage meaningfully with the art. The success of these pieces often hinges on balancing complexity with usability, ensuring they are both technologically sophisticated and user-friendly.

Moreover, AI installations have the potential to make art an educational tool. By engaging audiences in interactive, sometimes playful experiences, these works can inspire curiosity about both the art itself and the technology driving it. They offer a gateway for individuals to explore concepts such as machine learning, algorithms, and data processing, fostering a deeper understanding of contemporary innovations.

The educational impact of AI installations extends to how they promote conversations around the role of technology in society. By interacting with these pieces, audiences are encouraged to reflect on the broader implications of AI—its ability to influence culture, creativity, and daily life. This reflection leads to a more informed and thoughtful discourse about the rapidly evolving relationship between humans and machines.

Nonetheless, there's a delicate balancing act. Artists must negotiate the line between creating art that is genuinely interactive and art that feels overly orchestrated by the underlying technology. The magic of AI installations often lies in their ability to maintain this tension, offering an experience that's both controlled by machine intelligence and open to the randomness of human interaction.

In crafting AI installations, artists find themselves collaborating with technologists, engineers, and scientists, merging the traditionally separate domains of art and technology. This interdisciplinary approach fosters innovation, allowing for the creation of works that are more than the sum of their parts. The resulting installations are not just showcases of artistic skill or technological prowess but embodiments of the collaborative spirit that defines our current age.

Future developments in AI technology promise to further enhance the capabilities of interactive installations. As AI becomes more sophisticated, artists will be able to explore new forms of interaction and deeper levels of engagement. This evolution will continue to challenge conventional notions of what art can be, building a bridge to uncharted creative territories.

Ultimately, AI installations encapsulate the transformative potential of technology in the realm of art. They offer engaging, interactive experiences that are reshaping how audiences relate to art and each other. In doing so, they invite us to reimagine what it means to create and appreciate art in a world increasingly intertwined with intelligent machines. As these installations continue to evolve, they will undoubtedly inspire artists and audiences alike to explore the endless possibilities of AI-driven creativity.

Integration into Public Spaces

As AI-powered installations become increasingly prominent in the realm of interactive art, their integration into public spaces invites both intrigue and debate. Public spaces have historically served as the epicenters of cultural exchanges, evolving narratives, and artistic experimentation. Introducing AI into these environments transforms them into dynamic interfaces, where art and technology coalesce to create experiences that are both unexpected and deeply immersive.

The presence of AI in public art installations is not merely about adding a layer of technological sophistication. It's about crafting experiences that engage people in ways traditional art cannot. Imagine a sculpture that responds to the emotions of the crowd, altering its colors and shapes in real time, or a mural that evolves through its interaction with passersby, capturing moments in an ever-changing digital canvas. These aren't just concepts; they are realities enabled by the synergy of art and artificial intelligence.

Urban landscapes are ripe for these kinds of transformations. Local governments and cultural organizations increasingly recognize the value that AI art brings to public spaces. These installations can revitalize urban environments, turning mundane locations into vibrant cultural hubs. By utilizing AI, artists are no longer limited by the constraints of static media. They can create pieces that interact, reflect, and even converse with their surroundings and audiences.

The interactive nature of AI art in public areas doesn't just enhance aesthetic appeal; it also fosters community engagement. When art responds to and interacts with its viewer, it creates a unique dialogue that is engaging and personal. This dialogue encourages active participation, making viewers co-creators in the art process. As a result, the art experience becomes more inclusive, inviting diverse interpretations and emotional responses.

Furthermore, integrating AI into public art challenges preconceived notions about access and exposure to art. Public installations are accessible to everyone, regardless of socioeconomic background, education level, or familiarity with traditional art. AI's role in these spaces democratizes art, making it a shared communal asset rather than a privilege reserved for the few. This accessibility also brings art into the daily lives of people, encouraging artistic literacy and appreciation from an early age.

However, the introduction of AI into public spaces doesn't come without challenges. One of the main concerns is the technological complexity and maintenance these installations require. Ensuring they remain operational and engaging over time involves ongoing technical support and expertise. Moreover, there's a critical need to address privacy concerns, especially in installations that collect data or images from the public. Transparency about what data is collected and how it is used is crucial to nurturing trust between the creators and the audience.

Despite these challenges, the potential benefits of AI public art installations far outweigh the hurdles. As they continue to proliferate, artists, technologists, and policymakers must collaborate to balance innovation with ethical considerations. This collaboration is essential to fostering environments where AI art can thrive without compromising public trust or individual privacy.

Innovative partnerships between municipalities, tech companies, and artists have begun to set the groundwork for this balance. Initiatives focused on interdisciplinary collaborations are driving the development of public art projects that are not only aesthetically pleasing but also resonate with communities on a cultural and emotional level. By prioritizing public engagement and feedback, these projects can evolve more responsively, ensuring they meet the needs and expectations of their audiences.

The educational potential of AI in public art is another compelling aspect. These installations serve as live examples of how AI can be used creatively. They can inspire curiosity about the technology behind them, prompting learning and exploration among all age groups. School groups, families, and individual visitors can learn about AI's impact through workshops, guided tours, and interactive sessions linked to the art installations, sparking inspiration and future interest in technology and the arts.

As the relationship between AI and public spaces deepens, it's essential to remember that the ultimate goal is not to rely solely on technology for creativity but to enhance human experiences through it. AI should be seen as a tool that empowers artists, enriches cultural landscapes, and transforms public spaces into living canvases of human expression.

Future trends suggest that AI in public spaces will move towards even more personalized and context-aware installations. These pieces might incorporate advanced AI capabilities to understand and interact with the environment and audience in increasingly sophisticated ways. The collection of real-time data on crowd movements, environmental changes, and emotional responses will likely lead to art that dynamically adapts and evolves.

Ultimately, the integration of AI into public spaces represents a pivotal moment in the history of art and technology. As we continue to explore and expand upon these possibilities, it is crucial to foster an environment of inclusivity, transparency, and creativity. By doing so, we not only redefine what art can be but also how it can serve as a bridge between technology and society.

Chapter 25:
Sustainability and AI in Art

In the delicate tapestry of creativity and technology, the intersection of AI and art holds an exciting yet challenging promise. As AI plays an increasingly pivotal role in shaping artistic landscapes, the urgency to address its environmental footprint becomes paramount. The energy required to train complex AI models, coupled with the digital infrastructure they necessitate, often results in significant ecological impact. Yet, this challenge sparks innovation, driving artists, technologists, and industry leaders to explore sustainable solutions. From optimizing algorithms to require less computational power to utilizing renewable energy sources, the commitment to eco-conscious creativity is growing. This isn't merely a technical adjustment; it's a cultural shift, reminding us that art's progress should not come at the expense of the planet. By harnessing AI responsibly, we can ensure a future where artistic innovation and sustainability harmoniously coexist, inspiring not just new creations but a mindful dialogue on preserving our world.

Environmental Impact of AI Technologies

The rise of artificial intelligence in art presents both awe-inspiring possibilities and complex challenges, not least of which are its environmental implications. As AI technologies advance, they increasingly demand resources, computational power, and energy. At the core of this environmental concern is the massive energy consumption required for training AI models, which can be staggering in its volume. The carbon footprint left by AI processes, particularly those driven by deep learning algorithms, is significant and represents a growing environmental issue as these technologies proliferate in creative industries.

One of the main culprits of this energy consumption is the process of training deep learning models. This process involves feeding copious amounts of data through multiple iterations to fine-tune models, requiring sophisticated hardware and substantial electricity. For instance, training a single large transformer model can emit as much carbon dioxide as the lifelong emissions of several cars. This unsustainable demand for energy highlights a crucial area of concern for creatives deploying AI in their artistic endeavors.

Moreover, the hardware needed for such computations, often high-performance GPUs and specialized AI hardware, exacerbates electronic waste. The lifecycle of these devices—from production to eventual disposal—contributes to environmental degradation, especially when outdated equipment isn't properly recycled. As businesses and artists continuously upgrade to more advanced technology, the problem of electronic waste is set to increase unless there is a significant shift towards more sustainable practices.

There is growing interest in developing eco-friendly AI solutions within the art community. Efforts are focused on designing algorithms that are not only powerful and innovative but also efficient in their energy use. Researchers are exploring ways to optimize models to require less data processing and lower computational power, thus reducing the overall energy footprint. Techniques like model distillation, which simplify complex models into more efficient ones without significant loss of capability, are being actively researched.

An emergent field called green AI advocates for the consideration of power efficiency and carbon emissions in the development of artificial intelligence systems. By prioritizing energy-efficient models, developers hope to create systems that weigh the benefits of technological advancement against their ecological impact. These efforts recognize that striking a balance between creativity and sustainability is essential for the future of AI in art.

On a practical level, artists and developers are increasingly aware of their environmental responsibilities and are exploring ways to mitigate the impact of their work. Some initiatives focus on the use of renewable energy sources to power AI operations, like solar or wind energy, which offset much of the carbon footprint associated with traditional electricity consumption. This approach not only decreases emissions but also aligns with broader trends in sustainable art practices, which emphasize the use of green materials and processes.

Educational efforts are vital in fostering a culture of sustainability within the AI-driven art community. These include integrating environmental ethics and resource management into AI and art curricula, encouraging new generations of artists and developers to take environmental concerns seriously in their work. This shift in educational priorities could prove crucial in embedding sustainability into the ethos of AI art creation from the ground up.

It's not just about reducing the environmental impact of the technology itself, but also about leveraging AI to raise awareness and drive change. Artists are using AI to create works that comment on climate change and environmental degradation, harnessing the capabilities of the technology to visualize complex data in new and compelling ways. Such works not only highlight the issues but also catalyze discussions about technology's role in both causing and solving ecological problems.

The collaborative potential between AI developers and environmental scientists also presents a unique opportunity. By working together, they can innovate ways to incorporate environmental considerations into AI design processes. This might include developing AI that can monitor and manage resources more effectively or create systems that support environmental sustainability across different creative disciplines.

As AI continues to transform the creative industries, the drive towards sustainable practices isn't just a commendable goal; it's a necessity. In art, as in many fields, AI's vast potential needs to be harnessed thoughtfully to ensure it contributes positively to the world rather than causing inadvertent harm. The journey toward integrating these technologies sustainably is just beginning, but with conscious effort and collaboration, a more responsible, eco-conscious creative landscape can emerge.

In conclusion, while AI technologies have the capacity to redefine the artistic domain, they come with considerable environmental challenges that cannot be overlooked. By focusing on sustainable practices, from energy-efficient models to innovative collaborations, the art community can navigate the delicate balance between technological advancement and ecological stewardship, ensuring that creative exploration does not come at the expense of our planet.

Sustainable Practices in Creative AI

As the integration of artificial intelligence in art and creative industries grows, so do concerns about its sustainability. The environmental footprint of AI, alongside its transformative power, needs to be addressed thoughtfully. Sustainable practices in creative AI are essential, not just to lessen ecological impacts but also to maintain the integrity and ethical considerations of AI-generated art.

Environmental aspects are paramount when discussing sustainability in creative AI. The energy consumption of AI, particularly in training large neural networks, is considerable. This power use can contribute to a significant carbon footprint, challenging the efforts towards a sustainable future. With rising energy demands due to more advanced models, creativity in AI must consider its environmental implications, prompting a crucial dialogue on how to improve energy efficiency.

Strategies for reducing environmental impact include the development of more efficient algorithms and hardware. Researchers and engineers are focusing on creating AI systems that require fewer computations and operate effectively on less energy-intensive hardware. By innovating in this direction, they aim to create more sustainable frameworks that support the expansive capabilities of AI while being environmentally responsible.

One approach is through *edge computing*, which processes data locally rather than relying on centralized data centers. By harnessing the computing power on the edge of the network, creative AI applications can reduce latency and energy consumption, thereby mitigating some environmental concerns associated with AI's energy requirements. This is promising for artists and creators who wish to deploy AI solutions without a heavy environmental cost.

There is also a growing trend towards utilizing renewable energy sources in data centers as companies and organizations strive to supply their energy-hungry AI models sustainably. Creative industries can take inspiration from such initiatives and work towards applying similar practices in their production processes. Commitment to using renewable energy not only supports sustainability goals but also enhances the brand's reputation as a forward-thinking and environmentally conscious entity.

Moreover, sustainable practices in creative AI aren't solely about energy efficiency and environmental concerns. It also involves ethical production processes that respect labor rights and promote inclusivity. In developing AI models for creative purposes, it is critical to ensure fair labor practices for individuals and communities involved in the data collection and annotation processes. The sustainability of AI in the creative sector is a holistic endeavor that balances environmental, social, and governance (ESG) factors.

Efficient resource management goes hand-in-hand with AI-driven creative projects. AI models rely heavily on vast datasets, which sometimes include sensitive or personal information. Preserving the anonymity and rights of data contributors is essential. Creators employing AI tools should adhere to stringent data governance policies that protect users' privacy and set industry standards for ethical data usage.

In addition to data ethics, sustainability demands consideration of broader social impacts. AI in art can influence perceptions and prompt societal shifts, demanding responsibility from creators to promote positive social change rather than perpetuate bias or inequality. This involves conscious efforts to train AI on diverse data sets and avoid reinforcing stereotypes, thereby supporting a more inclusive creative expression.

Sustainable practices in creative AI also encourage the adoption of transparent methodologies. Open access to AI models, code, and datasets can contribute to a more sustainable ecosystem by enabling collaboration and reducing redundant efforts. When resources are shared, AI technologies can be iterated upon in ways that lead to more efficient, less resource-intensive models. This transparency fosters an environment where creativity and sustainability can thrive hand in hand.

Artists and creatives must be active participants in this sustainability narrative. As primary users of AI in arts, they wield significant influence in shaping industry standards and practices. By advocating for sustainable use of AI—not just in conversation, but through actionable practices—they can lead the cultural shift towards more environmentally and ethically sustainable creative industries.

Creative AI can act as a catalyst for sustainability in art, transforming both the process and the products of creativity. When artists leverage AI's capabilities thoughtfully, they can produce works that comment on and inspire environmental consciousness. This can generate dialogue and raise awareness about sustainability issues, prompting audiences to consider their own roles in environmental stewardship.

Innovative partnerships can further bolster sustainable efforts. Collaborative efforts between technology companies, environmental scientists, and the arts community can drive the development of tools and frameworks that prioritize sustainability without sacrificing artistic ingenuity. Such interdisciplinary collaborations are crucial in establishing a holistic approach to creative AI sustainability.

The journey towards sustainability in creative AI is ongoing and demands continuous evaluation and adaptation. As technology evolves, so too must our strategies for ensuring an environmentally and socially responsible impact. Artists, creators, developers, and consumers all have roles to play in this ecosystem, advocating for practices that support a sustainable and equitable creative future.

By embedding sustainability into the fabric of AI-driven art, we champion not only technological advancement but also social responsibility. Through concerted efforts, the convergence of creativity and AI can flourish sustainably, inspiring future generations to pursue innovation with an ethical and green conscience. This vision for creative AI doesn't just protect our planet, but also enhances the cultural richness of our shared human experience.

Conclusion

The narrative of artificial intelligence reshaping the creative landscape is not just about technology or art, but a profound merger of imagination, innovation, and the unknown. Through this exploration, we have traversed a rich tapestry of ideas where creativity and technology meet, collide, and eventually harmonize. What stands out prominently is AI's capacity to extend our creative capabilities far beyond conventional boundaries, inviting us to redefine creativity itself.

AI challenges our preconceived notions about originality and authenticity. By acting as both a mirror and a muse, it offers new dimensions for artists and creators to explore. While traditional art forms stand resilient, AI is both a competitive force and a collaborative partner, amplifying our human potential. This fusion enables us to transcend the limitations of human imagination, breathing new life into art forms and crafting unprecedented experiences.

An intriguing consequence of AI's integration into creative processes is the redefinition of artistic identity. As machines become generative partners, the line between creator and creation blurs. Artists find themselves in a symbiotic relationship with technology, where machine-generated ideas fuel human innovation and vice versa. This partnership compels a re-examination of the role of the artist, shifting from solitary genius to facilitator of unique interactions between code and canvas, algorithm and artistry.

The ethical implications of AI in art also beckon attention. As technology becomes a co-creator, questions of authorship, ownership, and moral responsibility emerge. Who owns a piece of art created by an AI? Who can claim the rights to music composed by an algorithm? These are questions that challenge legal norms and require soul-searching as we navigate this uncharted territory. The ethical dimension is not merely legalistic but ultimately philosophical, prompting us to consider the very nature of creation and the essence of what makes us unique.

In this interconnected world, cultural shifts driven by AI ripple across global art movements, affecting everything from local traditions to international collaborations. AI's role in erasing geographical limitations allows artists from diverse backgrounds to converge on digital platforms, creating a richer tapestry of global artistic exchange. The democratization of tools enables broader participation in the arts, fostering diversity in voices and perspectives.

Looking forward, AI's trajectory in the creative realm is shaped by possibilities as awe-inspiring as they are unpredictable. As technology evolves, so too does the canvas upon which creativity is drawn. We can anticipate further breakthroughs in how AI intersects with human creativity, offering new tools, methods, and philosophies. This will undoubtedly question our traditions but also inspire new forms of expression yet to be conceived.

The cultural implications of AI are far-reaching, shaping not just the art world but society as a whole. As AI continues to challenge and redefine creativity, it beckons us to reconsider our relationship with technology and, in turn, with one another. The potential for AI to inspire innovation is boundless, coaxing us to push beyond known limits and into the realm of the previously unimaginable.

Concluding this journey, we stand at a crossroads teeming with potential. This is not the end but a new beginning, a launchpad for further exploration into the transformative role of AI in art and media. For the creative professionals, industry leaders, and tech enthusiasts among us, the invitation is clear. Embrace the possibilities, explore the intersections, and continue to forge paths where creativity and technology converge to redefine what is possible. The canvas is yours—make it unparalleled.

Appendix A:
Resources and Further Reading

As we journey through the evolving landscape of AI and creativity, it's clear that we stand at the edge of another revolution in artistic expression. The fusion of machine intelligence and human creativity is a rich and vast territory to explore, and the following resources will provide deeper insights and expanded perspectives on this fascinating field.

Books and Articles

"The Creativity Code: Art and Innovation in the Age of AI" by Marcus du Sautoy - This book delves into how machines are expanding the boundaries of creative thought and the ethical questions that arise.

"Artificial Intelligence: A Guide to Intelligent Systems" by Michael Negnevitsky - Offering a comprehensive look at AI technologies, this text provides foundational knowledge useful for understanding AI's role in artistic fields.

"Deep Learning for Creativity" by Norah Smith - An insightful read on how deep learning models can emulate human-like creativity in art and music.

"The Singularity is Near" by Ray Kurzweil - While not solely focused on creativity, Kurzweil's book contextualizes AI's rapid growth and innovation across various domains.

Academic Journals

The Journal of Creative AI - This journal focuses on the intersection of AI and creative practice, offering research papers that examine the latest innovations.

AI & Society - A journal exploring the impacts of AI on society, including cultural and creative implications.

Online Resources

AI Webinars and Podcasts - Platforms such as Coursera and edX offer free webinars on AI in creative industries. Podcasts like "Talking Machines" give listeners continual updates on AI advances.

CreativeAI.net - A community hub for sharing AI-created art, this site provides inspiration and collaboration opportunities for AI enthusiasts and artists.

Conferences and Workshops

NeurIPS Conference - Noted for its coverage of machine learning advancements, NeurIPS also includes discussions on AI applications in creative fields.

AI for Creatives Summit - A specialized symposium dedicated to exploring AI's role in artistic innovation, featuring keynote speakers from around the globe.

Research Organizations

OpenAI - Renowned for its cutting-edge research, OpenAI explores the capabilities and implications of AI across multiple sectors, including the arts.

The AI Art Lab - Dedicated to merging technology and creativity, this lab supports research and experimentation in digital and algorithmic art.

These resources serve as a gateway for anyone eager to dive deeper into the ever-expanding realm of AI-driven creativity. Engaging with these materials will not only enhance your understanding but also inspire new ways of thinking and creating as we navigate this technological renaissance together.